LIFE OF JESUS

Also by John Dickson

The Best Kept Secret of Christian Mission:
Promoting the Gospel with More Than Our Lips

The Christ Files: How Historians Know
What They Know about Jesus

LIFE OF JESUS

WHO HE IS AND
WHY HE MATTERS

JOHN DICKSON

ZONDERVAN®

ZONDERVAN.com/
AUTHORTRACKER
follow your favorite authors

ZONDERVAN

Life of Jesus
Copyright © 2010 by John Dickson

This title is also available as a Zondervan ebook.
Visit www.zondervan.com/ebooks.

Requests for information should be addressed to:
Zondervan, *Grand Rapids, Michigan* 49530

Library of Congress Cataloging-in-Publication Data

Dickson, John.
    Life of Jesus : who he is and why he matters / John Dickson.
       p.   cm.
    ISBN 978-0-310-32867-4 (softcover)
    1. Jesus Christ — Person and offices. 2. Apologetics. I. Title.
BT203.D54   2010
232'.8 — dc22   2010018074

Cover design: LUCAS Art & Design
Cover images: Allan Dowthwaite, Paul Moss, Mal Hamilton, and John Dickson
Interior design: Melissa Elenbaas

Printed in the United States of America

HB 04.09.2018

FOR MARK CALDER
With thanks for years of friendship
and collaboration in the great task

CONTENTS

PART 4

JUDGE AND FRIEND

JESUS' THOUGHTS ON "RELIGIOUS HYPOCRITES" AND "ROTTEN SINNERS"

PART 5

CROSS EXAMINATION

JESUS' DEATH AS THE SOURCE OF LIFE

PART 6

THE RESURRECTION

HOW COULD IT HAPPEN? WHAT DOES IT MATTER?

DISCUSSION GUIDE FOR THE SIX-SESSION VIDEO CURRICULUM

ACKNOWLEDGEMENTS

THANK YOU:

to my colleagues at the Centre for Public Christianity for the amazing effort put into the *Life of Jesus* project, and especially to Dr. Greg Clarke for the conversations which form the background to some of the more interesting material that follows, and to Simon Smart for assistance with the curriculum questions

to Kate Wilcox for excellent suggestions about the first two chapters

to Jenny Glen for tireless attention to detail

to Dr. Ann Eyland for much-needed assistance extracting accurate statistical data for chapter one

to my wife, Buff, for editorial assistance

to Matthias Media for the use of *The Essential Jesus* translation of Luke's Gospel and for years of partnership together

to my sceptical friends – you know who you are – for listening to my material over the years and helpfully challenging me at every point

to David and Alison Whalley for years of hosting the courses that evolved into *Life of Jesus*

THE WAY WE BELIEVE

(or What I Learnt from Aristotle)

THREE HUNDRED YEARS BEFORE CHRIST, THE GREEK PHILOSOPHER
Aristotle made an observation about you and me that I think
has stood the test of time. In his book *On Rhetoric* he laid out
a theory about how people form their beliefs, that is, how they
come to be persuaded by political, religious, ethical and cultural
argument. His work, incidentally, was literally the textbook on
persuasion for the next two thousand years, right up until the
eighteenth century. Long before our post-modern love of decon-
structing viewpoints and seeing through media spin, readers
of Aristotle delighted in learning from one of history's greatest
minds about why some messages seem compelling to us and others do not.

Aristotle said that people form their beliefs on the basis of a
combination of three factors: what he called *logos*, *pathos* and
ethos. *Logos* is the intellectual dimension, the part in us (or in the
argument we are listening to) that corresponds to logic and common sense. As rational beings we like to know that our beliefs are
generally factual, reasonable and grounded in something other
than wishful thinking. I'm sure most of us would agree so far
with the great Athenian philosopher.

But it is a foolish person, Aristotle argued, who thinks we
form our beliefs *only* on the basis of intellect. In addition to *logos*
there is *pathos*, the personal or emotional dimension of belief that
is just as real as the rational part. An argument with *pathos* is one
with a beauty and poignancy that resonates with our deepest self.
A message of this kind meets our passions and longings. Don't
misunderstand me. Aristotle was not talking about mere frivolous
artistry. He hated what he called mere "sophistry" – a message
that was all style and no substance. Part of the reason he wrote

11

his book was to criticize this form of persuasion. Nevertheless, Aristotle was adamant that there was a good *pathos*, in which a well-made argument also corresponds to our perfectly reasonable expectation that what is true should also be attractive and personally satisfying. This is another way of saying that people rarely change their minds on big issues based only on information.

Finally, there is *ethos*, the social dimension of persuasion. What we believe is hugely influenced by our upbringing, our education and the circle of friends we find ourselves in. It is part of our human nature to accept more readily the views of people we know, admire, trust and love. In Aristotle's own words: "we believe fair-minded people to a greater extent and more quickly than we do others on all subjects in general and completely so in cases where there is not exact knowledge but room for doubt."[1] Since the 1960s this has been known as the "sociology of knowledge" –the way our social context informs and frames our perspective– but Aristotle put his finger on it millennia ago.

Take climate change. How do we form our views on this fraught topic? It would be unrealistic to assume that you and I hold our respective views based on facts alone (*logos*). Professional climate scientists aside, most of us do not have firsthand knowledge of the data. We become climate change believers or deniers not just because of formal evidence but also because of personal (*pathos*) and social (*ethos*) factors. On the one hand, those of us with slightly activist temperaments or "apocalyptic" personalities will find ourselves drawn toward dramatic climate change scenarios. On the other hand, those who like a good conspiracy theory will easily suspect that the guild of climate change scientists has some ulterior motive in presenting its case. This is *pathos* at work. More simply, chances are we all find ourselves influenced by social factors on this question (*ethos*). Our political bias, the university we attended, the friends we talk to about the topic –each of these will have had some impact on our thinking.

What's this got to do with the life of Jesus –the man and why he matters? Put simply, on a topic as complex and far-reaching as this we ought to acknowledge that our current beliefs –whether positive or negative– will have developed partly through *logos*, partly through *pathos* and partly through *ethos*. No one embraces faith in Jesus Christ based solely on factual evidence. Equally, no one rejects Christianity or loses his faith solely because of (a lack of) facts. A combination of intellectual, personal and social factors is at work.

What I find so interesting as I ponder Aristotle's insight is the way contemporary believers readily admit the multifaceted nature of their faith. When Christians talk about how they "became Christians," they will often mention an intellectual component, a personal component and a social component. They will talk about some book they read or sermon they heard that laid out the facts about God and Christ. Their intellect was nourished and impressed. But they will also happily tell you, for example, how one day while pondering the significance of Jesus they felt a deep resonance with the Christian gospel. The message somehow became attractive and personally satisfying. It answered deep longings and clarified certain confusions. And very often such people will admit to having been drawn into a community of Christians, at school, church or wherever, whose lives had an authenticity and goodness that was hard to argue with.

But what I find especially fascinating is the way many sceptics of religion today will not admit that they are sceptics for the same combination of reasons. Instead, they claim to resist Christianity for logical reasons only. There is not enough proof for the reality of God, they say. Books and documentaries on Jesus have undermined his uniqueness or even existence. "I would believe," I have heard my sceptical friends say, "if only you gave me some proof."

I don't doubt that evidence is important to many people. So it should be. (Personally, I'd give up Christianity tomorrow if I thought the facts stacked against it.) But I do doubt that this is the only factor in people's unbelief–or even that it is always the main factor. I have had too many conversations over the years with avowed "atheists" who, after some deeper discussion and growing friendship, admit that their reasons for resisting Christ are more complex than first acknowledged. An event in the past called into question the fairness or existence of the Almighty. A Christian they once knew turned out to be an ugly hypocrite and it spoiled their appreciation of anything coming out of the mouth of believers. Personal and social factors prove important for unbelief, after all.

The point of all this is to ask readers, whether Christian or not, to explore the life of Jesus fully aware that we form our views on the big questions (and the small ones) through a range of factors. We are complex people. We are intellectual, emotional and social beings, and each of these components plays some part in how we respond to material like this. I will definitely be laying out what seem to me quite robust arguments for the life and significance of Jesus, but I have no intention of hiding the fact that some of what follows appeals to the personal and social dimensions of our lives. After all, if there is a God, surely we should expect his truth not only to be factually verifiable but also personally satisfying and socially relevant.

PART 1

GOD'S SIGNPOST

Jesus as a Tangible Sign of God's
Interest in Our World

PART GOD'S SIGNPOST

CHAPTER 1

THE GOD-QUESTION

THE WORLD IS A VERY RELIGIOUS PLACE, AND THE MUCH-HERALDED renaissance of scepticism dubbed the "new atheism" is unlikely to change things. An important minority of Westerners identify as atheists, but it is much smaller than the publicity suggests. The last World Values Survey (2005–06), the most reliable data set available, found that 10.4 percent of Britons, 9.9 percent of Australians, 7 percent of New Zealanders and 3.6 percent of Americans accept the tag "atheist."[1] And even these numbers may be inflated. In 2008 Olivera Petrovich, an expert in the psychology of religion at the University of Oxford in the UK, caused a stir by presenting empirical evidence that infants naturally incline toward belief in some kind of Creator; atheism, in other words, is *not* the default position. More relevantly, in a recent interview for the *Centre for Public Christianity* (CPX) she outlined research revealing that respondents describing themselves as "atheist" in surveys do not necessarily deny the existence of God. A significant proportion of them admit in post-survey analysis that the tag "atheist" functions

The magnificent spirals of the nearby galaxy Messier 81 are highlighted in this NASA Spitzer Space Telescope image.

Courtesy of NASA

more as a protest against formal religion than a description of their disbelief in any kind of god.[2] Openness to the divine is more dogged and widespread than we sometimes realize.

Even in my own country, which has often been described as the first *post*-Christian society in the world, surveys continue to reveal very high levels of spiritual, and specifically Christian, belief. Sixty-eight percent of Australians believe in a God or a Universal Spirit, and 63 percent believe in the possibility of miracles today.[3] Slightly more than that (75.9 percent) believe that Jesus himself performed miracles (while only 6 percent think he never existed).[4] Most surprising for those of us who live in this supposedly godless country, when asked to rate out of 10 "How important is God in your life?" (1 being "not important at all" and 10 being "very important"), 57.4 percent of Australians selected 6 and above; 28 percent selected 10.[5]

Despite the fact that atheist writers such as Richard Dawkins and Christopher Hitchens are on the bestseller lists worldwide, the larger point remains: the world is a very religious place. For most people throughout most of human history the stunningly rational universe we see *out there* and the uncannily rational mind we experience *within* suggest the existence of some kind of divinity or Deus responsible for this reality. (I'll discuss in a moment whether this Deus is an *impersonal Mind* or a *personal God* involved in the affairs of the world.)

PERCEIVING GOD

I am not trying to prove the existence of the Deus or God. This is not that sort of book, nor do I think it is really possible. Frankly, I am trying to get the God-question out of the way, so I can focus on the history and relevance of Jesus. I offer these comments simply to point to the near-universal human belief in some kind of divinity. Put simply, most of us perceive in the physical world and in ourselves a larger *intention*. The whole thing seems arranged, not accidental; created, not a product of chance. And so we imagine there must be a Creator. The ancient Hebrew poet describes the sentiment well:

> The heavens declare the glory of God;
>   the skies proclaim the work of his hands.
> Day after day they pour forth speech;

night after night they display knowledge.
They have no speech, they use no words;
   no sound is heard from them.
Yet their voice goes out into all the earth,
   their words to the ends of the world.[6]

The same point was made by St Paul in his hugely influential Epistle to the Romans: "Since the creation of the world God's invisible qualities – his eternal power and divine nature – have been clearly seen, being understood from what has been made."[7] Belief in God, in other words, is not a deduction people make only after analyzing evidence and weighing arguments. It is far more basic, more instinctive. It is something most of us *perceive directly* by living in a world that seems strangely rational in the way it is put together. This is not to deny that countless professional philosophers go beyond this intuition to provide sophisticated arguments for belief in God.[8] All I am saying here is that the *perception* seems to be a fundamental thing for most of us, which is probably why infants, whether in Britain or Japan (where Dr Petrovich did her comparative research), work out themselves that the world was made by "someone."

I realize that some people do not "perceive" these things. I am not sure I have an adequate explanation for this, other than to point out that some of humanity's *other* grand ideas also sometimes go unacknowledged. Some people dislike music, for instance, and others hate art. I cannot explain this. Plenty of people are anarchists too. They honestly believe that cultural mores, ethical standards and systems of government are bad things, mere inventions that hinder human flourishing. I puzzle over why they do not perceive the truth and beauty found in some form of "rule." I am not suggesting a connection here between atheism and anarchism or between atheism and disdain of the arts. I am just observing that some ideas can be fabulously compelling to most thinking people and *not* at all obvious to a minority of equally thoughtful people. Intellectually, I puzzle over atheism just as I puzzle over anarchism and a-artism.

At this point, my atheist friends like to throw in a favourite rhetorical flourish: "You Christians reject all the gods of history except one – we atheists just deny one god more." The suggestion here is that when Christians reflect on why they reject Zeus, Ra, Isis, Vishnu, et al., they will come to see the good sense of the atheist who simply adds one more deity to the rubbish bin.[9] This is cute and repeated surprisingly often, but a moment's thought shows it to be rather silly. For one thing, believers in any particular religion do not reject other gods *in toto*. They deny only the particular manifestations and stories of the other deities. A Christian, for instance, can happily acknowledge the wisdom of the ancient Egyptians or Indians in positing the existence of a powerful Intelligence that orders the universe, whether Ra or Vishnu, and then beg to differ with these ancient cultures when it comes to the elaborations and add-on characteristics of these particular gods. There is an irreducible conviction shared by all worshipers: the rational order of the universe is best explained by the existence of an almighty Mind (or Minds) behind it all. Atheists, then, are simply wrong to liken their rejection of all divinity to a Christian's rejection of particular versions of divinity.

The analogy of marriage might help. True, I have rejected all other potential spouses in favour of my darling Buff, but this does not mean I have rejected the idea at the core of everyone else's marriage. It would be a rather zealous celibate who ventured to say, "When you consider why you reject Amelia, Michelle and Heather (the wives of some of my colleagues at CPX), then you will see the good sense of rejecting marriage altogether; we celibates just go one partner further." As if the difference between committed monogamy and deliberate celibacy is one of degree! There is a huge difference between my rejection of particular marriage partners and the celibate's rejection of marriage itself. There is an equally large difference between a Christian's denial of particular manifestations of the divine and an atheist's rejection of divinity itself. It will take more than neat rhetorical flourishes to undermine the tenacious, near-universal conviction that there must be some kind of Deus behind our world.

COMMONSENSE DEISM

Where believers of the various faiths part ways is in the *particularization* of the Deus. While I can happily endorse the logic behind a deity like Vishnu–that a powerful, intelligent being preserves the universe–I cannot see a good reason to believe, for example, that Vishnu appeared (as the avatar Krishna) to Prince Arjuna on the eve of his great battle with the Kauravas to strengthen him and disclose the paths of salvation. This story comes from the Bhagavad-Gita and, unless I already accept the authority of this sacred Hindu text, I fail to see how I can accept its claims as true. The story doesn't provide a unique answer to any outstanding philosophical question, so its explanatory power is limited. Nor is there any historical data confirming Arjuna's visitation or his battle or even his existence. I am left with no reason to accept this particular manifestation of divinity, even though I concur with my Hindu friends that there must be some mighty, preserving Being behind the universe. On the reality of a Deus we agree, but as we start telling stories about this Being we go our separate ways.

This is probably the place to flag the philosophical distinction between *deism* and *theism*. Deism accepts that there is a powerful Mind behind the universe, but it stops short of saying anything descriptive about that Deus. A *soft* deist would simply plead ignorance about the personal qualities of the Deus; a *hard* deist would insist the Deus has *no* personal qualities as such: people who say they believe in a "universal spirit" probably fall into this latter category.

Theism, on the other hand, from the Greek word for "god" (*theos*), is deism *plus*. It accepts the core conviction of deism that behind the rational world lies a rational Mind, but it goes further, insisting that some things *can* be said about the Deus. In a sense, religions begin with the assumption of deism and then move beyond it to theism as they start talking about the Deus as benevolent, righteous or angry, or that it has spoken in some sacred text, or that it has revealed itself in history, or that it can hear our prayers, and so on.[10] Here, the Deus is thought of not in impersonal terms but as a thinking, personal Theos.

With all due respect to committed atheists, it seems to me that deism is the only responsible conclusion one can draw from simply pondering the uncannily rational nature of the universe. Whether the Deus cares for us, what its moral views are, whether it hears our prayers, whether it guides human history—i.e., whether the Deus is a Theos—are second-order questions that lie beyond simple rational observation of the physical world. Please don't misunderstand me: personally, I am a theist not just a deist. But I will happily acknowledge that my theism rests not on rational observation of the physical world but on other factors I will discuss in a moment. What I am saying is that thoughtful reflection on the origin and nature of existence will lead you only as far as deism, i.e., to the conviction that behind the orderliness of nature and the corresponding rationality of the human mind must lie some immense Mind.

Albert Einstein was a deist, so far as we can tell from his own statements and from those who knew him. He rejected both theism and atheism, preferring to acknowledge some kind of eternal spirit whose rational nature was imprinted on the physical universe (he frequently used the word "God" but only in this nebulous, deistic sense).[11] Other famous physicists, such as Prof Paul Davies of Arizona State University (formerly of Australia), also admit to something like deistic views. Davies even wrote a book called *The Mind of God* in which he openly discussed his conviction that the order of the world and, in particular, the emergence of our own rational minds cannot have been an accident but were in some meaningful way *intended*.[12]

I sometimes wonder if even the avowed atheist Richard Dawkins is sympathetic to some form of deism. "My title, *The God Delusion*," he writes, "does not refer to the God of Einstein and the other enlightened scientists of the previous section.... In the rest of this book I am talking only about *supernatural* gods" (original emphasis).[13] Einstein was critical of atheism just as he was critical of personal theism, so I am left wondering what exactly Dawkins is approving and disapproving of here.[14] Whatever the case, recently an even more influential sceptic than Dawkins moved from atheism to overt deism.

Antony Flew, former professor of philosophy at the University of Keele (and Reading) in the UK and author of a number of important textbooks on philosophical atheism, including *God and Philosophy* and *The Presumption of Atheism*,[15] has been as influential among professional philosophers as Dawkins has in the general public. But in 2007 he surprised many by publishing *There Is a God: How the World's Most Notorious Atheist Changed His Mind*.[16] Actually, Flew stops short of saying he believes in "God" in the personal sense, but he is clear that "the three items of evidence we have considered in this volume—the laws of nature, life with its teleological organization, and the existence of the universe—can only be explained in light of an Intelligence that explains both its own existence and that of the world."[17]

Christians were jubilant, almost claiming Flew as a convert; atheists were outraged, suggesting the professor's old age had got the better of him. Neither is appropriate. Flew had just joined the commonsense ranks of the vast majority of people throughout history in perceiving that the rationality of the universe and of our own minds can only be explained by the existence of some sort of divinity. Deism is common sense.

CHAPTER 2

THE OBVIOUS NEXT QUESTION

IF DEISM IS THE COMMONSENSE POSITION, WHY BOTHER GOING further and speculating about the nature and involvement of the Deus? Why not just feel the occasional moment of awe and reverence toward "it" and get on with life? Do we really have to enquire into whether the Deus is a Theos? Part of the answer is this: it's the obvious next question. If there is a great Mind behind the universe, common sense compels me to ask whether (and what) that Mind *thinks* and, in particular, whether (and what) it thinks of *us*. Sure, I may reject all the answers currently on offer, whether concerning Krishna or Jesus or whatever; I may even decide the question is beyond human knowing. But it is still a sensible question. And most cultures have had a go at answering it.

The question of whether the Deus is actually a personal Theos cannot be answered by mere rational observation of the universe. This is not like looking at the orderliness of nature and the rationality of the human mind and concluding that Intelligence is a better explanation of our existence than coincidence. It is not a

Buddhist temple

scientific problem at all; it is a *personal* and *historical* question. It is more like asking *Does my wife truly love me?* or *Did Alexander the Great really reach India?* Science contributes little to such discussions. But does this mean I cannot still arrive at confident answers to both questions (in the affirmative)? No. In the first case I rely on personal experience of my wife. While this will not be probative for those who do not share my experience, it is nonetheless utterly compelling to me. In the second case I rely on multiple ancient sources that tell me about Alexander's exploits in India. These two ways of knowing – personal experience and historical testimony – are perfectly adequate paths to drawing firm conclusions. Neither is "scientific" in the normal sense.

What has this got to do with God? Many people "sense" God personally. They find themselves getting to know him in a way analogous to befriending someone. Here, things like meditation, personal prayer, reading Scripture and the transformation of their moral and emotional life convince many that God is truly present in their lives. They have personal knowledge. Of course, talk like this will not convince those who have not experienced such things; sceptics often scoff at claims of "religious experience." But for people who have actually felt the divine in this way, it provides a very compelling reason to think that the Deus is a Theos. The great Mind they *intellectually* know to exist is encountered in daily experience *personally*. Whole books have been written on this personal dimension of knowing God (only some of which I would recommend[1]). This is not one of them.

But what about the *historical* dimension of the God-question? Beyond personal experience, we might also look for some indication on the world stage that the Deus has touched Earth in a public, tangible way. Evidence of such a divine-human encounter would provide grounds for thinking that God was interested in us. It would give us a reason for moving from deism to theism, from a rational intuition that the universe was intended to a warranted belief in a personal God. This involves *historical* questions more than scientific ones.

Science can only really test what is observable and/or repeatable: chemical reactions, fossil records, cosmic background radiation and so on. But, almost by definition, historical events are unobservable and unrepeatable: Alexander's march to India;

Pontius Pilate's execution of Jesus; the mugging of a certain Dionysius, son of Zoilus, at the bath-house of Aristodemus.[2] The vast knowledge of Einstein, Davies, Dawkins and Flew combined could not adjudicate on evidence of God's involvement *in history*, since such evidence would have little to do with universal constants; it would involve historical particulars. The brilliance of an Einstein or a Davies might confirm our suspicion that atheism is very probably false and that the universe was in fact "arranged," but scientific expertise cannot help us assess whether Krishna appeared to Arjuna on the plains of Kurukshetra or whether Jesus lived, taught, healed, died and rose again in first-century Palestine. Such things are said to have happened at particular times and particular places. That means we are looking not for a verifiable principle of mathematics or a theory testable in a lab but for a "dent" in the historical record matching the claims. We are looking for independent sources written close in time to the purported events by people sufficiently free of impure motives. This is exactly how we know that Alexander reached India. It is an important part of assessing claims about God acting on the stage of human history.

THE ODD THING ABOUT JESUS

This book explores the daring claim made by the world's two billion Christians. Uniquely among the great faiths, Christianity goes out on a limb by making claims that can, to a significant degree, be investigated historically.

All religions claim some sort of "revelation." Buddhism depends on the profound insights gained by Siddhartha Gautama (the Buddha) during his moment of enlightenment while meditating under a Bodhi tree. Hinduism looks to the Vedas passed on to the first man at the dawn of time. Islam says that the angel Gabriel dictated to the Prophet Muhammad the very words of God.[3]

But Christianity claims something very different. At the heart of the world's largest faith is not a lone spiritual insight, a mystical story from the dawn of time or a dictation of divine words in a holy book, but a series of events that are said to have taken place in public, in datable time, recorded by a variety of witnesses. For better or worse, Christian Scripture is fundamentally different from other holy books. In the events of Jesus' life, death and resurrection believers claim to observe a tangible, testable sign directing us to the "kingdom of God." Christians are therefore claiming to possess not just a dogma–a set of divine truths–but a verifiable history. As a result, the beliefs and texts of Christianity become uniquely open to public scrutiny. It is as if Christianity places its neck on the chopping block of academic scrutiny and invites anyone who wishes to come and take a swing. Which is why historians and biblical scholars of all religious (or nonreligious) persuasions in universities around the world feel at liberty to view the Christians' holy book, the New Testament, as a simple *historical* text.

Let me illustrate the difference this makes to our search for evidence of God's involvement in the affairs of the world. Imagine that the rest of *Life of Jesus* were an exposition of a revelation I received in a dream in which my great, great grandfather spoke to me about the true nature of divinity, the mysteries of the afterlife and the proper way to conduct my life. How would you judge (a) whether I really did experience the dream and (b) whether the content of the dream was true? Part (a) you could only take on trust. By definition, a dream is imperceptible to all but the one who experienced it; independent corroboration is impossible. How would you assess part (b), the content of the dream? You could take the subjective path and just see if what my great, great grandfather taught resonates with you, whether it feels right. But what if my divine disclosure did not immediately resonate with you: could you still make an assessment of the truth or falsehood of its content? It is difficult to see how. Without some "this-worldly" sign supporting the truthfulness of the dream's content, it cannot be verified. And so you are left with the subjective assessment: does it *seem* true? Many religious conversions operate at this instinctive level. People hear a message (or are brought up hearing it), and they find that it fits with their personal situation or meets some felt need. So they accept it as truth. (People reject faith or drift away from it for equally subjective reasons.)

Many religious claims are as immune to external testing as my hypothetical dream concerning the Dickson patriarch. Did Prince Arjuna see Lord Krishna and learn from him the highest path of Bhakti or devotional religion? We cannot rule it out.

But nor can we apply any objective assessment. As I said, this story comes to us in the Bhagavad-Gita and has no historical corroboration. We may read the Hindu scriptures and find them speaking to us of eternal truths, but we cannot point to any near contemporary Indian text or archaeological evidence confirming the battle on the plains of Kurukshetra or the existence of Arjuna, let alone the appearance of Krishna. The Bhagavad-Gita itself is not even written in historical prose. It is a poem. All hope of identifying historical sources within the text—a normal part of the scholarly analysis of Tacitus or the Gospels—must be abandoned.

Please don't misunderstand my point. I am not criticizing my Hindu friends or even saying that their stories are false. Indeed, they cannot be proved false. I am making the broader philosophical point that the claim at the heart of the Bhagavad-Gita cannot be tested in any external way. The appearance of Krishna to Arjuna turns out to be an *a*-historical claim that can be believed only by taking it on faith.

Isn't Christianity in the same position? Yes and no. Much of the Bible is as untestable as the Krishna story. Millions of people believe it and feel that God speaks to them through it, but if they are asked "What is the evidence that God revealed himself to Abraham?" or "How do you know the book of Revelation reveals the future?" Christians usually reply, "I just do" or "It makes sense to me" or "I know it in my heart." I do not dismiss the validity of this approach. If God has revealed himself in a book, you would expect it to resonate in this manner. The problem is, that doesn't help those looking for a reason external to faith to accept the Bible as true.

That said, there is one portion of the Bible that is historically verifiable to a high degree, and it happens to be the central part of the story. The life of Jesus is completely unlike Abraham's epiphany or the visions of Revelation. It is in a category altogether different from Krishna's appearance to Arjuna. Jesus *has* left a dent in the historical record, and a significant one. The central claims about him belong to the same category as the claims about Alexander reaching India. We can test them. We have data and methods, external to personal faith, for demonstrating the events of Jesus' life.

WHAT WE KNOW CONFIDENTLY

As we will see throughout this book, the vast majority of scholars investigating Jesus – whether Christian, Jewish or atheist – are confident about the following historical details: Jesus was born during the reign of emperor Augustus; grew up to be a famous teacher and healer in Galilee; called a small group of disciples; scandalized the religious leadership by closely associating with "sinners"; clashed with the Jerusalem elite over his sharp criticisms of the temple; was arrested, tried and crucified by the Roman prefect Pontius Pilate; and, shortly afterward, was declared by his first followers to be the Messiah risen from the dead. All of this we can affirm without recourse to religious faith. We have enough sources close in time to the events themselves to declare *at least* these things to be historical fact, and only someone employing avoidance strategies would dispute them.

Many of the great public universities of the world, such as Oxford and Cambridge in the UK or Harvard and Yale in the US, offer undergraduate and postgraduate units on New Testament and early Christianity. Such courses are not theology in the confessional sense found in seminaries and theological colleges, but considered biblical studies, the historical analysis of Christian Scripture free from dogmatic constraints. Sometimes you even find courses in classics or ancient history departments on such topics as New Testament history and the historical Jesus. Australia's largest department of ancient history, at Macquarie University, offers no fewer than eight units on Jesus, Paul, the New Testament and early Christianity.

My earlier analogy of a dreamlike revelation does not apply to the story of Jesus. A more appropriate illustration might run like this. Imagine I came to you claiming that my late great, great grandfather revealed himself not in a dream but in Times Square, New York, last Monday during the morning rush hour. His appearance stopped the traffic and left witnesses dumbfounded as he explained to them the truth about the spiritual realm. Leaving aside the comical nature of the analogy, the claim itself is one you could test to some degree. You could watch the news services, read eyewitness accounts, check the New York traffic reports and so on. You might not be able to prove it beyond all doubt, since there is always room for scepticism about things you have not personally experienced, but a fair-minded person would be able to arrive at a reasonable judgement about its truth or falsehood. You would be able to decide whether the claim is supported by the kind of evidence you would expect if such an event had taken place. If you found no evidence at all, you would be well within your rights to dismiss it. If you found good evidence, or at least more evidence than you would expect if the story were a fiction, then you could quite rationally accept it as true. This is what I mean by a testable claim.

The central claims of Christianity are to a degree testable. You can apply the normal tests of history – the same ones applied to Alexander's campaign in India – and find that we do in fact possess exactly the sort of evidence you would expect if the core of the Jesus story is true and decidedly more evidence than you would expect if the story were fabricated. The evidence is not probative, so sceptics still have plenty of wiggle room. But the dent in the historical record is significant enough for any fair-minded person to accept that, whatever its explanation and significance, the life of Jesus really looks as though it took place in much the way the Gospels say it did.

The reason for pointing all of this out is to underline that in the claims about Jesus we have a reasonable indication that the God of our hunches has touched the earth in a tangible way. His story is the kind of thing you would expect to find if God really were interested in us. It is a story that not only resonates at the personal and cultural level – which is why so many think of Jesus as the most influential figure of history – but one that, objectively speaking, looks as though it is true. I remain a devoted theist rather than a commonsense deist because I am convinced that the great Mind standing behind the rational order of the universe has entered into human affairs in a concrete way in the life of Jesus. (I also freely admit to experiencing God personally through my reading of the Bible, answered prayer and the slow but real transformation of my life under the influence of his presence.) Of all the religious claims in the world, I believe that Jesus' life provides interested observers with the most plausible, externally testable reason for moving beyond intellectually respectful deism to a heartfelt (but no less intellectual) theism.

I again call Prof Antony Flew as witness. In the main part of *There Is a God* Flew simply outlines how an avowed philosophical atheist came to join the vast majority of men and women in believing in "a self-existent, immutable, immaterial, omnipotent, and omniscient Being"[4]–in other words, a Deus. But at the back of that book (Appendix B) there is an extraordinary little essay by the British biblical scholar and Bishop of Durham, N. T. Wright, whom Flew invited to pen something on the historical nature of Jesus. Flew explains, "If you're wanting omnipotence to set up a religion, it seems to me that this is the one to beat!"[5] He says he still has doubts about the resurrection of Jesus, but he admits that if such a thing as a tangible revelation from God exists, Jesus is the best candidate. I hope I am not misrepresenting Antony Flew's position when I say that these opening chapters and his closing one share a similar line of reasoning. There is a Deus: the strikingly rational laws of nature and the uncannily rational capacity of human minds to comprehend those laws are best explained by the existence of an immense Intelligence behind the universe. Whether or not that Deus has revealed itself to the world is the next obvious question, and the claims about Jesus of Nazareth provide the most compelling affirmative answer available.

Flew admits to a certain excitement about this possibility,[6] but he remains undecided about the reality. Of course, I go further. I am not just excited but confident that Jesus is God's tangible disclosure. He is exactly what interested observers need in order to confidently move from a vague acknowledgement of the divine to a sincere trust in a personal God. What follows in *Life of Jesus*, then, carries somewhat more significance than if this were a *Life of Alexander* (as interesting as that would be). In the events of Jesus we find God himself publicly at work in the world. That is the basic claim of Christianity. Once we get going in our historical analysis, the God-question will fade into the background a little. But this cannot obscure the fact that whenever one investigates the figure of Jesus, life's most profound questions sit invitingly in the corner.

CHAPTER 3

EVIDENCE FOR JESUS

PEOPLE COULD BE FORGIVEN TODAY FOR THINKING THAT SERIOUS biblical scholars believe that most of the details of Jesus' life are either completely unknown or totally contrary to what Christians affirm. Neither is true.

It is difficult to convey just how vast contemporary scholarship on Jesus really is. Leaving aside works of Christian theology and technical commentaries on biblical books, the number of scholarly volumes on the historical figure of Jesus is huge, though I would say the *essential* works, those constantly discussed in the scholarly literature, number around 100. In the library of Macquarie University where I teach there are well over 200 books on the historical Jesus—"theology" is not taught at this institution—more than for any other figure studied in our Ancient History Department, eclipsing Alexander the Great and Julius Caesar combined. Then there are the academic journal articles relating to the Jesus of history. These would run to many thousands.

Excavated part of the pool of Siloam

I would venture to say that no other figure of history–ancient or modern–has nearly the number of scholarly books and articles dedicated to analyzing his life and teaching. I realize this does not prove much (other than that many scholars find him very interesting), but it does underline the difficulty facing anyone trying to distill Jesus scholarship for popular consumption. It also highlights the intellectual disrespect shown to academia by those who glibly deny Jesus' very existence.

I recently had a very awkward conversation with a politician here in Australia who is also a vocal sceptic. She told me in passing that Jesus probably did not exist. "But there is some pretty good evidence," I suggested. "No there isn't," she replied. "It's all fabricated." I took a deep breath and came back once more, "Are you telling me that all those ancient historians and biblical scholars investigating the historical Jesus in universities around the world are misguided?" Without embarrassment she retorted, "If they spend their time studying myths, yes!" There was nowhere to go after that.

WHAT KIND OF EVIDENCE ARE WE LOOKING FOR?

But what kind of evidence should we expect to find for a figure like Jesus, and how ought we to assess it? I have written a couple of other books on these questions,[1] so I hope you will allow me to give just the briefest account of the sources and methods employed by experts of the historical Jesus.

The first thing to hold in mind is the sheer randomness of the historical record. Only a tiny proportion of the buildings and writings of the first century has survived–perhaps less than 1 percent. We have shopping dockets from lowly peasants of the first century and yet not one piece of personal correspondence from Emperor Tiberius, the man who ruled the world in Jesus' day. Scholars have to draw their conclusions from the flotsam and jetsam that history throws up.

There are many examples of the haphazard nature of historical evidence. The Gospel of John refers to a public bath in the Siloam district of Jerusalem–Jesus is said to have performed a healing there. But archaeological digs throughout the city failed to discover such a pool. Some scholars began to doubt the pool ever existed; others claimed that the story was only meant to be metaphorical. Then, in June 2004, during sewerage works in the district of Old Jerusalem, workers accidentally uncovered steps that led down to a huge public bath, dated to the time of Jesus. It is without doubt the missing pool of Siloam. Overly sceptical writers were suddenly embarrassed. They had wrongly supposed that the uncorroborated pool never existed.

The town of Nazareth provides another case. All four Gospels agree that Jesus' Galilean hometown was Nazareth: "[Jesus] went to Nazareth, where he had been brought up" (Luke 4:16). Over the years, sceptics have declared this town a fiction, primarily because Josephus, a Jewish writer from the first century and a one-time resident of Galilee, did not mention Nazareth among the nearly fifty other towns and villages named in his works. The sceptical assumption here was this: only things *outside* the Gospels count as evidence. But then archaeological digs in the 1950s uncovered remains of an ancient village on the traditional site of Nazareth. Cisterns, silos, wine and olive presses and tombs were all found. It was estimated that the town was small, with a population of no more than 2,000 – which probably explains why Josephus did not mention it.[2]

So then the sceptics tried to insist that the remains did not pre-date the Roman-Judean war of AD 66–70. (This is what you call an avoidance strategy.) The same was argued when in 1962 an inscription was found on a marble wall of a third–fourth century synagogue referring to a priestly family that had relocated to Nazareth.[3] Doubters hung on to the notion that this cannot have been a Nazareth that existed in the early first century; the Gospels had it wrong. (I should clarify here that this scepticism was not coming from serious scholars, only from anti-Christian activists.) Then, on December 21, 2009, the Israel Antiquities Authority, the governing body for excavations throughout Israel, announced the discovery of a small house in Nazareth. The official dating of the house (based on pottery remains and the like) is *early first century*. "The discovery is of the utmost importance since it reveals for the very first time a house from the Jewish village of Nazareth," said chief archaeologist at the site, Yardenna Alexandre. "Until now, a number of tombs from the time of Jesus were found in Nazareth, however no settlement remains had been discovered that were attributed to this period."[4] Sceptics must give up forever the attempt to deny the existence of Jesus' hometown.

The discoveries of the pool of Siloam and the house at Nazareth underline a very basic principle of historical investigation: *absence of evidence is not evidence of absence.* Just because something is reported in only one or two sources does not mean it is spurious. With only 1 percent of the literary and physical data from the first century in our possession we should be very slow to dismiss.

JESUS IN PASSING

As it turns out, the evidence for Jesus is slightly better than historians might have predicted. The randomness of history has worked in our favour here. Jesus was a relatively minor figure in his immediate day. Yes, he came to be worshipped by two billion people, but in his day he was a virtual nobody outside the administrative backwater of the Roman empire that was Judea and Galilee. Most Roman officials would never have heard of a Jesus of Nazareth until the movement in his name began to pick up momentum. It is frankly surprising that Jesus rates four clear mentions in passing in non-Christian writings from the period.

The Stoic writer Mara bar Serapion (about AD 75) refers to Jesus as a king, teacher and martyr. He does not mention Jesus by name but, overwhelmingly, contemporary scholars regard this as an important, if veiled, reference to Jesus of Nazareth:

> What good did it do the Athenians to kill Socrates, for which deed they were punished with famine and pestilence? What did it avail the Samians to burn Pythagoras, since their country was entirely buried under sand in one moment? Or what did it avail the Jews to kill their wise king, since their kingdom was taken away from them from that time on? God justly avenged these three wise men. The Athenians died of famine, the Samians were flooded by the sea, the Jews were slaughtered and driven from their kingdom, everywhere living in the dispersion. Socrates is not dead, thanks to Plato; nor Pythagoras, because of Hera's statue. Nor is the wise king, because of the new law which he has given.[5]

The Roman historian Tacitus (writing about AD 115) is probably the most important historical source for the period from

Caesar Tiberius to Nero (AD 14–68). He confirms the execution of Jesus by order of the Roman governor Pontius Pilate. He does so only in passing while explaining to his readers how the recently founded group known as Christians, whom Nero had blamed for the great fire of Rome, got their name:

> Nero substituted as culprits, and punished with the utmost refinements of cruelty, a class of men, loathed for their vices, whom the crowd styled Christians. Christus, the founder of the name, had undergone the death penalty in the reign of Tiberius, by sentence of the procurator Pontius Pilatus, and the pernicious superstition was checked for a moment, only to break out once more, not merely in Judaea, the home of the disease, but in the capital itself, where all things horrible or shameful in the world collect and find a vogue (Tacitus *Annals* 15.44).[6]

This is a surprising piece of evidence. "Tacitus is very clear," says Prof Alanna Nobbs, head of the Department of Ancient History at Macquarie University. "He is writing about emperors. He is writing about warfare, at home and abroad. He is writing about Rome and the provinces. He is not terribly interested in a minor province and what to him would have been a very minor figure within that province." She concludes, "To my mind, and many of my colleagues would agree with me, it is unusual to have so much devoted to Jesus."[7]

A Jewish writer delivers a similar "highlights" package. Josephus commanded troops in Galilee three decades after Jesus. Toward the end of the century (around AD 90), he wrote up a history of his Jewish people in which he makes passing mention of a man called Jesus–twice:

> And so he [the High Priest Ananus] convened the judges of the Sanhedrin and brought before them a man named James, the brother of Jesus who was called the Christ, and certain others. He accused them of having transgressed the law and delivered them up to be stoned (Josephus, *Jewish Antiquities* 20.200).[8]

The New Testament also mentions "James, the brother of the Lord" but, whereas the book of Acts leaves off with this James alive and well in Jerusalem around the year 57,[9] Josephus helpfully informs us what happened to him five years later in AD 62. Like his more famous brother three decades earlier, James died a martyr's death at the instigation of the Jerusalem elite. The very offhand nature of the mention of Jesus – simply to reference the lesser-known James – heightens the significance of the passage as evidence for Jesus' existence in first-century Palestine.

Josephus also mentions Jesus two sections earlier. The reference is again very much in passing (he is discussing the deeds and misdeeds of Governor Pilate), but at least here we get some details about the man:

> About this time there lived Jesus, a wise man. For he was one who wrought surprising feats and was a teacher of such people as accept the truth gladly. He won over many Jews and many of the Greeks. When Pilate, upon hearing him accused by men of the highest standing amongst us, had condemned him to be crucified, those who had in the first place come to love him did not give up their affection for him. And the tribe of the Christians, so called after him, has still to this day not disappeared (Josephus, *Jewish Antiquities* 18.63–64).[10]

This passage is frequently dismissed as a complete forgery by people committed to denying the historicity of Jesus. This is the result of people misconstruing the scholarly conversation about the text. Most scholars, including those with a specialty in Josephus, believe that a scribe *added* words to the original paragraph sometime in the middle ages. With the three agreed additions, which I deliberately did not include in the quotation above, the text reads:

> About this time there lived Jesus, a wise man, *if indeed one ought to call him a man.* For he was one who wrought surprising feats and was a teacher of such people as accept the truth gladly. He won over many Jews and many of the Greeks. *He was the Messiah.* When Pilate, upon hearing him accused by men of the highest standing amongst us, had condemned him to be crucified, those who had in the first place come to love him did not give up their affection for him. *On the third day he appeared to them restored to life, for the prophets of*

God had prophesied these and countless other marvellous things about him. And the tribe of the Christians, so called after him, has still to this day not disappeared.

It is very difficult to imagine a non-Christian Jew writing such things about Jesus, so it is best to think of these statements as attempts to bring Josephus' rather neutral statement about Jesus into line with Christian feelings. Only the most idiosyncratic scholars have imagined the whole paragraph is a forgery. The style is very much that of Josephus and several lines in the original paragraph are unlikely to have come from a Christian hand. For example, what Christian would say Jesus "won over many Greeks" when the Gospels explicitly say otherwise? What Christian would describe the figures behind Jesus' execution as "men of the highest standing"? More importantly, until the modern age no one had thought to suggest Jesus was not an actual historical figure. So, while it is easy to imagine a Christian scribe "improving" what a Jewish writer had written about Jesus, it is anachronistic to imagine him inventing a proof for something no one at the time disputed. Virtually every serious scholar in the field regardless of religious affiliation would agree with Prof Graham Stanton of Cambridge University: "Once the obvious interpolations are removed this paragraph gives an ambivalent or even mildly hostile assessment of Jesus – one which can be attributed to Josephus with confidence."[11]

WHY NO SERIOUS SCHOLAR DOUBTS JESUS' EXISTENCE

Doubts about Jesus' existence are still occasionally raised by those engaged in polemics against theology rather than participation in academic history. But it is not regarded as a serious line of enquiry in the secular, historical study of the man from Nazareth. One searches in vain for articles in the peer review literature questioning Jesus' existence, because any such attempt would involve an attack on historical knowledge itself. If we know anything about anyone from the ancient world, we know that Jesus lived and died in first-century Palestine. Speaking of our three passages above, Profs Gerd Theissen and Annette Merz of the University of Heidelberg in Germany – leading critical scholars and by no means advocates of Christian apologetics – write:

The mentions of Jesus in ancient historians allay doubt about his historicity. The notices about Jesus in Jewish and pagan writers in § 3 above–especially those in Josephus, the letter of Sarapion and Tacitus–indicate that in antiquity the historicity of Jesus was taken for granted, and rightly so.... All three know of the execution of Jesus.... The execution was offensive for any worship of Jesus. As a "scandal" it cannot have been invented.[12]

But this is not where scholars leave the matter, as the following chapter will make clear.

THE MOST IMPORTANT SOURCES FOR JESUS ARE THOSE LEFT BY HIS followers – the books now found in the New Testament.

All texts have blind spots and points to prove. Historians are not trying to find sources without an agenda – as that would leave us with virtually nothing, ancient or modern. Instead, they try to analyse each and every source in the light of its obvious point of view. This is how scholars read every ancient text, including the Gospels.

Historians, in other words, do not privilege the New Testament texts, as Christians do, but nor do they approach them with sceptical prejudice. The Gospels are treated like any other historical text of the first century, whether those of Tacitus or Josephus. Christians may be unsettled by this "secular" approach to their sacred texts, but sceptics will find no comfort here either. The fact is, mainstream experts overwhelmingly agree that the core of the gospel narrative is historically sound. Let me bear this out with a famous quotation. Anyone acquainted with historical Jesus

The oldest fragment of the New Testament from the Gospel of John

studies will know the name Ed Parish Sanders, a longtime professor at Duke University and, in everyone's estimation, one of the most important scholars of the last thirty years. He is no friend of traditional Christianity, but his statement of what can be known about Jesus from an historical analysis of the Gospels has stood the test of time:

> There are no substantial doubts about the general course of Jesus' life: when and where he lived, approximately when and where he died, and the sort of thing that he did during his public activity.... I shall first offer a list of statements about Jesus that meet two standards: they are almost beyond dispute; and they belong to the framework of his life, and especially of his public career: Jesus was born c. 4 BCE, near the time of the death of Herod the Great; he spent his childhood and early adult years in Nazareth, a Galilean village; he was baptized by John the Baptist; he called disciples; he taught in the towns, villages and countryside of Galilee (apparently not the cities); he preached "the kingdom of God"; about the year 30 he went to Jerusalem for Passover; he created a disturbance in the Temple area; he had a final meal with the disciples; he was arrested and interrogated by Jewish authorities, specifically the high priest; he was executed on the orders of the Roman prefect, Pontius Pilate.
>
> We may add here a short list of equally secure facts about the aftermath of Jesus' life: his disciples fled; they saw him (in what sense is not certain) after his death; as a consequence, they believed that he would return to found the kingdom; they formed a community to await his return and sought to win others to faith in him as God's Messiah.[1]

"BIOGRAPHIES" OF JESUS

One thing we know for sure. While the Gospels have an obvious agenda – to convince people about Jesus – they are also strongly *biographical*, real accounts of a real life that cannot be read simply as metaphors of spiritual themes.[2] The historical-biographical nature of the Gospels is particularly clear in the opening paragraph of the Gospel of Luke, a text written within living memory of Jesus and the main focus of our tour through his life:

Many have attempted to put together an account of the things that have been fulfilled among us, just as these things were passed on to us by those who from the beginning were eyewitnesses and servants of the message. For this reason, it seemed good to me as well, having investigated everything thoroughly from the start, to write something orderly for you, Most Honourable Theophilus. My aim is that you may know the certainty of the message you were taught (Luke 1:1–4).

A word or two about Luke might be important here. Luke was well placed to write a history of Jesus. Apart from being well educated (something we can discern from the quality of his Greek), he wrote within living memory of Jesus, probably in the mid–70s AD. He was also personally acquainted with several of the key eyewitnesses to Jesus' life, including the apostle Paul and James. Occasionally today it is claimed that the early church wrangled over which Gospels to include in the New Testament, the final choice being driven by political outcomes. The evidence tells a different story. From the very beginning, just four biographies of Jesus were acknowledged to have come from the first century, that is, the period of the eyewitnesses. They are the Gospels of Matthew, Mark, Luke and John, now in the New Testament. It is true that some second- and third-century texts were written in the name of eyewitnesses (e.g., the Gospel of Thomas, the Gospel of Judas), but these did not enjoy the wide acceptance of the earlier Gospels, and were written far too long after Jesus (a century or more) to contain reliable information, according to most scholars today. The Gospel of Luke, on the other hand, was held in high esteem amongst the early Christians because of its careful research and explicit reliance on the testimony of eyewitnesses. As we read Luke's account of the life of Jesus, we are in good hands.

Returning to Luke's opening paragraph above, the dedication is to a "most Honourable Theophilus." It was quite common in Luke's day to dedicate works to high officials or patrons. The opening lines of Josephus' *Against Apion*, for instance, written about twenty years after Luke, begin: "In my history of our Antiquities, most excellent Epaphroditus, I have, I think, made sufficiently clear the extreme antiquity of our Jewish race."[3]

Unfortunately, we have no idea who Luke's "Theophilus" was. We know who Luke himself was–as I just said, he was a traveling companion of the apostle Paul and an acquaintance of key eyewitnesses to Jesus from at least the year AD 49.[4] The best we can say about Theophilus is that he was some well-respected individual–"most honourable" may suggest he was a Graeco-Roman official of the kind Luke would have met in his travels with Paul. He may even have been the patron of the project.

KEYS TO READING THE GOSPELS

Whatever the identity of Luke's dedicatee, these verses are not just a dedication but a kind of literary key that unlocks the whole Gospel. In fact Luke gives us three keys to reading his work. First, nothing could be clearer than that he intends his Gospel to read as an historical account of historical events. He insists that his material comes ultimately from eyewitnesses.[5] Notice also the way Luke places his work alongside numerous other accounts known to him when he wrote (probably in the AD 70s): "Many have attempted to put together an account of the things that have been fulfilled among us." Most scholars are fairly sure we know of at least three sources known to Luke (and used by him): about 60 percent of the Gospel of Mark, written in the late AD 60s, appears almost verbatim in Luke; the other two sources[6] contain many of the sayings and parables of Jesus. Analysis of Luke's Gospel reveals a basically conservative approach to these sources: he was committed to preserving material about Jesus rather than making it up.[7]

In stressing the historical dimension of Luke I do not want to suggest he was a dispassionate journalist reporting facts for facts' sake. The life of Jesus *is* history, but it is also much more than history. It is the culmination of a backstory, so to speak, the fulfillment of a grand heritage predating Jesus by millennia. That heritage, of course, is the history and prophecy of the Old Testament, the Jewish Scriptures. This is the second key to reading Luke's Gospel, and he strikes the theme in a single (but crucially important) word: "the things," he says, "that have been *fulfilled* among us."

The point here is that we will not be able to understand the history of Jesus unless we also pay attention to the backstory found in the Old Testament. John the Baptist's dunking people in the Jordan River (Luke 3), for example, only comes alive when we remember that Israel entered into the Promised Land centuries earlier by wading through *the Jordan River*. Jesus' selection of twelve apostles (Luke 6) seems like an arbitrary number until we recall that there were twelve tribes of ancient Israel. Suddenly, we see that Jesus was on a kind of renewal program. Again, Jesus' talk of the kingdom of God (Luke 9–11) makes little sense without appreciating that a thousand years earlier King David had been promised a descendant who would reign over an eternal kingdom. And, finally, Jesus' death on a cross (Luke 23) would be just another martyrdom were it not for the powerful Old Testament idea of a sacrifice for sins bringing mercy to God's people.

One of the enormous differences between our New Testament Gospels, written in the first century, and the so-called Gnostic Gospels, written in the second and third centuries, is the way the former are so rooted in the Jewish Scriptures. Whereas the New Testament Gospels stay true to the irrefutable historical reality that Jesus was a Jew thoroughly steeped in the Jewish Scriptures, the Gnostic writings purge the Jesus-figure of all such Jewishness. In fact, their Jesus is rather anti-Semitic, believing the God of the Old Testament to be a lesser and, ultimately, deceitful deity from whom Jesus came to deliver us. I know it has become fashionable in popular conversations about Christianity to treat the Gnostic Gospels as of equal importance to the Gospels of Matthew, Mark, Luke and John. Richard Dawkins even goes so far as to suggest that the Gospels that did make it into the Bible "were chosen, more or less arbitrarily, out of a larger sample of at least a dozen."[8] This is careless point-scoring from an otherwise thoughtful sceptic. A glance at the scholarly literature will reveal that most experts agree not only that the four New Testament Gospels were written in the first century but also that they were a fixed and authoritative collection by at least the middle of the second century, decades before most of the Gnostic Gospels had even been written (the only exception is the Gospel of Thomas, which was probably written around AD 120). There is no evidence that any of the Gnostic Gospels was even considered for inclusion in the New Testament. When the church councils met in the third and fourth centuries to discuss whether books such as Revelation, James, Jude and Hebrews should be ratified as part of the New Testament canon there was *no* discussion about the Gospels or the letters of Paul. These had long been accepted as totally authentic and authoritative for the church.[9]

My larger point here is that the theme of fulfillment is central to the Gospels. If we avoid paying attention to the background provided by the Old Testament, we will be left with an airbrushed Jesus, not the figure of history.

JESUS' STORY, OUR STORY

There is a third key to reading the Gospels. Luke makes clear in his introductory paragraph that his purpose is not just to tell us the *history* of Jesus and its *backstory*. He wants it all to connect with *our story*. There is, in other words, a personal dimension to the Gospels. As politely as he can, Luke tells his honoured dedicatee, Theophilus, that he would love to see him move on in his journey of faith: "My aim is that you may know the certainty of the message you were taught" (Luke 1:4). Theophilus obviously knew something of the Jesus story, but it is impossible to tell from Luke's language whether or not Theophilus was already a Christian, since the Greek term translated "taught" (*kat che*) can mean both "formal instruction" or simply "report/rumour."[10]

What is clear is that Luke would like to see Theophilus move from being merely taught to grasping "the certainty" of these things for himself. In the original language the word "certainty" is the last word of the sentence, which is one of the ways in Greek to emphasize an idea. Although it makes for bad English, Luke literally says, "that you may know concerning the message you were taught *the certainty*." This Greek term *asphaleia*, from which we get the modern construction term "asphalt," basically means "security" or "stability." Luke's point is not so much that he wants Theophilus to believe *more strongly* or *unwaveringly*, but for him (and us, all the years later) to be reassured of how strong and unwavering is the One in whom he has faith. In other words, Luke wants his readers, however strong or weak our faith, to grasp the security, stability, and dependability of the Jesus we meet in his account. Based on the rest of the Gospel, it is clear he wants us to see how firm are the connections between Old Testament prophecy and the fulfillment found in Jesus; to know the facts about Jesus' life, not just the popular imaginings about him; to fix our lives to the anchor of Jesus' teaching rather than the whims of contemporary culture; to feel the assurance of God's forgiveness of sins; and to rejoice in the hope of the kingdom Christ said would outlast all others.

This personal dimension of the Gospel writings should not be interpreted as an indication that these ancient writers were so agenda-laden they were incapable of truthful reporting. For Luke, as for the other Gospel authors, this material only matters to the extent that the events actually occurred in time and space and were passed on accurately by "those who from the beginning were eyewitnesses." And, in any case, the Gospel writers are at least upfront about their agenda. This is a real "plus" for historical interpretation, says classicist Prof Alanna Nobbs:

> We have to remember that all writers of any description
> have certain perspectives from which they are coming. Now,
> in the case of the New Testament, a big plus for us is that we
> know what the perspectives are. So, really, for a historian
> interpreting the New Testament writers, you do not have to
> go digging around for their motives. We know their motives.
> This does not, however, invalidate the things that they say.[11]

A LEAP IN THE DARK

Acknowledging the personal dimension of the Gospels does not diminish the factual aspect. Both go together in historical writing. Indeed, both factors combine in most of our really important life choices, including those involving faith, a much maligned and misunderstood concept.

In his book, *The God Delusion*, Richard Dawkins uses a dictionary definition of "delusion" as his definition for faith: "a persistent false belief held in the face of strong contradictory evidence."[12] That is the view of someone who is strongly opposed to religion, but even people who have more time for faith often think of it as believing something despite the evidence for it. Faith is a kind of wishful thinking, a hope that something is true when you do not have any good reason to think that it is.

On this understanding, faith and reason are opposites, and no rational person would say he or she has faith. But this definition of faith cannot be found in genuine Christianity. The image of faith as a complete "leap in the dark" has caught on in popular understanding, but it is encouraged neither in the Bible, nor in most churches I have had anything to do with.

Christians are, in fact, very interested in evidence and reasons. The way in which the narrative of Jesus is written in the Bible pays close attention to evidence, recording names and dates and places with care, compiling witness accounts of events and speeches, and looking for verification of extraordinary acts such as miracles. They were, of course, written at a time before carbon dating, lie detectors and DNA testing, but as ancient reporting, the Gospels show strong interest in evidence for one's beliefs.

A fairer definition of faith is "reasoned trust." Far from being a leap in the dark, it is a confident move forward after you have had a really good look at what is in front of you. There is a gap between what history can demonstrate and what Christian commitment involves; it is nowhere near as large as people sometimes imagine, but it is real. However, it has to be remembered that some of the biggest decisions we make in life are made without complete proof, without all the evidence we could wish for. Every day people make a big financial and emotional commitment when they buy a house or car, but even being well researched cannot fully ensure the many aspects you just have to "take on trust" from the previous owner, and what you get may not be what was advertised.

Or perhaps a more comparable example is marriage. People commit to marriage without knowing everything they would like to know about their potential spouse. The period of courtship cannot provide solid evidence that this person is the one with whom to spend your life "for better, for worse," etc. It can offer strong indications that two people are compatible, but it cannot produce proof. Does this make the decision to marry irrational? Some would say yes (perhaps on other grounds), but most would say no. The decision to marry is not a leap in the dark. Couples at that point do in fact know a lot about the person they are promising to love and cherish. They most likely (at least in Western-style relationships) have known the person for some time, have checked out their habits, learned about their life story and made assessments of their character. All of this provides a strong indication that the decision is a good one; and, usually, strong indication is enough to move forward in many life-changing choices.

Faith in Jesus is more like getting married than solving a mathematical proof. There is a great deal that we know about the life of Jesus and what it means to become a Christian, but it isn't a puzzle that we solve – it is a relationship that we enter.

There are, as with all relationships, some mysterious factors in what brings a person to profess a Christian faith: your upbringing, your previous convictions concerning religion, the experiences you have had, and even whether you want the Christian faith to be true. All of these things affect the process. You do not take the journey to faith in a vacuum; you do it with all of your own baggage, your own preferences, your own strengths and weaknesses, and your own desires. History provides a strong indication that the Jesus story is believable, but Christian faith is a richer and more complex thing than mere believability.

PART 2

CHRISTOS

The Identity of Jesus and His
Critique of "Religion"

CHAPTER 5

MORE THAN A SURNAME

MOST OF US HAVE A PARTICULAR PICTURE OF JESUS IN OUR HEADS. There is the 1970s Hollywood Jesus with blue eyes and long blond hair. There is Martin Scorcese's sexually unfulfilled, misunderstood prophet in *The Last Temptation of Christ*. There is Mel Gibson's more recent version in *The Passion of the Christ* where Jesus appears as a sacrificial lamb, the object of ninety minutes of cinematic brutality. There is the Jesus of left-wing politics who wouldn't hurt a fly, or the right-wing Jesus who probably would. Very recently Deepak Chopra, guru to the stars, gave us his *Third Jesus* in which this ancient Jewish teacher basically appears as an enlarged Indian guru – a projection of Chopra himself perhaps.

It is hard to know how to think of Jesus, especially since in the last few years we have seen a stream of blockbuster claims about him. One documentary claims to have found a secret Gospel written in the name of Judas, the betrayer of Jesus. Another tells us Jesus' tomb has been discovered, complete with evidence of his wife and family. It all sounds intriguing, but what is so

Jews at the wailing wall

often lacking in these portraits – including some of those offered by Christians – is historical evidence. So, let's begin with something simple – his name.

Our earliest piece of information about Jesus is a brief summary of beliefs scholars recognise as a creed that was being memorised and repeated by Christians within months of Jesus' death. The apostle Paul quotes the creed in his first letter to the Corinthians (15:3). It begins "*Christos apethanen*" or "Christ died." Within months of his death, Jesus was being hailed as "Christos" – "Christ."

Growing up in post-Christian Australia in a household that never went to church, I assumed "Christ" was a surname. People use the words "Jesus Christ" the way they might say "John Lennon" or "Bill Gates," so it seemed reasonable to me at the time that there would have been a Mary and Joseph Christ, Grandpa Christ and so on. Only later did I learn that "Christ" was a prestigious title – for two of the world's religions.

Each day, Orthodox Jews recite prayers for their long-awaited king: "Have mercy, our God, on Jerusalem your city ... on the monarchy of the house of David, Your Christ," or in Hebrew, *mashiach*, Messiah.[1] The word "messiah" means "anointed one" and is a reference to the coronation of ancient Israelite kings, each of whom was anointed with olive oil as a symbol of God's power being poured out. The model was King David, who reigned around 1000 BC. David was a shepherd-turned-warrior who was selected by God and *anointed* to rule Israel for a generation.[2]

The Jewish Scriptures, or what Christians call the Old Testament, promised that a descendant of this David would one day rule all the nations. Anointed not just with oil but with the measure of the Spirit of God, he would speak and act for God. A text written several centuries after David, at a time when the royal dynasty of David was in ruins, puts it this way:

> A shoot will come up from the stump of Jesse [David's family name];
>> from his roots a Branch will bear fruit.
> The Spirit of the LORD will rest on him –
>> the Spirit of wisdom and of understanding,
>> the Spirit of counsel and of might,

the Spirit of the knowledge and fear of the LORD –
and he will delight in the fear of the LORD.
He will not judge by what he sees with his eyes,
or decide by what he hears with his ears;
but with righteousness he will judge the needy,
with justice he will give decisions for the poor of the
earth.
He will strike the earth with the rod of his mouth;
with the breath of his lips he will slay the wicked....
In that day the Root of Jesse will stand as a banner for
the peoples; the nations will rally to him, and his resting
place will be glorious (Isaiah 11:1–10).

This deep Jewish longing for a Messiah descended from David helps us to appreciate the scandal at the heart of all four Gospels: in different ways they all claim Jesus is that anointed one, the Christ. He is the one to speak and act for God.

The problem was that Jesus did not fit the job description of the Messiah many in his day were expecting.

THE MILITARY MESSIAH

For most of the six centuries before Jesus, Israel was dominated by foreign super-powers: the Babylonians (sixth century BC), followed by the Persians (sixth–fourth centuries BC), then the Hellenistic (or Greek) empires (fourth–second centuries BC). There was a brief period of self-rule beginning with Judas Maccabeus in 164 BC but that came to an end in 63 BC when the Romans arrived. The Romans imposed heavy taxes and made their military presence felt throughout the region. The "holy land" was being trampled underfoot by unclean overlords.

The locals were not happy. Many Jews in this period longed for a saviour who would crush their occupiers and establish what they called "the kingdom of God." This was the task of the Messiah. One text called the *Psalms of Solomon* (not to be confused with the book of Psalms found in the Old Testament), written by Jewish teachers in Jerusalem shortly after the Romans arrived, puts it this way:

See, Lord, and raise up for them their king, the son of
David, to rule over your servant Israel in the time known

to you, O God. Undergird him with the strength to destroy the unrighteous rulers, to purge Jerusalem from gentiles who trample her to destruction; in wisdom and in righteousness to drive out the sinners from the inheritance; to smash the arrogance of sinners like a potter's jar.... There will be no unrighteousness among them in his days, for all shall be holy, and their king shall be the Lord Messiah.[3]

Some Jews even tried to preempt the Messiah's kingdom by confronting the Romans head on. In 4 BC the residents of Sepphoris, a stone's throw from Jesus' hometown of Nazareth, raided the palace armory and seized back the city. The Romans crushed the rebellion and razed the city to the ground. There would be no victorious "Christ" on this occasion.

It is against this background that we can safely say Jesus did not really fit with the military image of the Messiah that some of his contemporaries were expecting. Central to his teaching was the path of non-violence, love and humility. Consider these famous words of Jesus from Luke's Gospel:

Love your enemies. Do good to those who hate you.
Bless those who curse you. Pray for those who mistreat you.
If someone strikes you on the cheek, offer him the other
cheek as well (Luke 6:27–29).

The contrast with the *Psalms of Solomon*, just quoted, could hardly be greater. For Jesus, the kingdom of God requires love not vengeance, humility not national pride. It is a lesson we learn right at the beginning of his story.

HUMBLE BEGINNINGS

The traditional Christmas narrative strikes a rather unexpected note about this so-called Christ:

While Joseph and Mary were in Bethlehem, the time
came for her to have the baby. And because there was no
room for them in the inn, she used strips of cloth to wrap
him up, and a manger for his cradle. In that part of the
country, there were shepherds who stayed out in the fields
at night to keep guard over their flock. Without warning,
one of the Lord's angels appeared to them, and said to them,

"Today, a Saviour has been born to you in the city of David. He is Christ the Lord. And this will be the sign for you–you will find a child wrapped up in strips of cloth and lying in a manger" (Luke 2:6–12).

The sign of the Christ is a baby in a manger, an animal feeding area. Not a glorious beginning! Luke is setting up a theme we find in all four of the New Testament Gospels. Jesus is the Christ, but his kingdom is not about military or political power. The Christmas image of a baby in a manger challenges the expectation of a Messiah on his throne.

And when was the first Christmas? You would imagine the date of Jesus' birth is a no-brainer–AD 1, right? After all, that is how we got our calendar. But it is not so simple. The Gospels of Matthew and Luke agree that Jesus was born shortly before the death of Herod the Great, the Rome-appointed ruler of the Jews who, according to firm dates provided by the first-century writer Josephus, died in March or April 4 BC. So, Jesus must have been born shortly before that–most scholars think around 5 BC.

Naturally, this raises the question: how could Jesus have been born five years before himself? The answer is this: the man who gave us the calendar distinction between BC and AD was a sixth-century Italian scholar named Denis the Little. His calculation of *Anno Domini*, the year of the Lord, was out by about five years–not bad considering his limited sources.

SO MANY IMAGES OF JESUS

I began this chapter reflecting that there are so many different images of Jesus. Although most people revere him, some make up their own version of who he is to suit whatever they think is best. They take an aspect of his life and teachings and magnify it out of all proportion to prove their point. So we get the teaching that Jesus was an anti-capitalist and socialist, because he told his disciples to share their belongings. It is true that Jesus' disciples did share their possessions (you can read about it in Acts 2:42–47 and Acts 4:32–37). However, this is not the sum total of Jesus' teaching on money and wealth–it is too convenient to label Jesus a socialist. Or we get gentle Jesus meek and mild, with no reference to his anger at religious hypocrisy or his bravery when facing the Roman authorities.

As Christianity spread after the first century, different emphases developed with respect to how Jesus was portrayed. In medieval paintings of Jesus he is most often a baby suckling at Mary's breast, an image of innocence and harmlessness that sometimes distracts from the adult Jesus (who is the figure we know most about). Without a doubt, the most common image of Jesus in art is in his crucifixion, hanging with arms stretched out on a wooden cross (common simply because it is found in the majority of churches). Whilst this image depicts the central concern of the Christian faith—the meaning of the death of Jesus—it, too, is only one aspect of what we know about Jesus. Whether it is an ornate Baroque crucified figure on the wall of a Roman Catholic cathedral or a Salvador Dali hanging in a modern gallery, this single image of Jesus on the cross is still not enough to properly communicate who Jesus was and what he did.

But there's more: you can get tough-guy Jesus for men with four-wheel drives. Some Christian groups like to emphasise Jesus' ruggedness and capacity to "take on a challenge"; an image of Jesus as the powerful opponent of evil forces seems to appeal to some macho types. Or if you are less aggressively inclined, you can get pacifist Gandhi-like Jesus by playing around with the Sermon on the Mount. You can even conjure up a gay version of Jesus, as Elton John recently did,[4] if you twist his relationship with his male disciples.

The point is that none of these caricatures of Jesus is going to help us work out who he really is. They are largely constructed from ideological foundations, to serve a predetermined purpose rather than to portray fairly what we know of Jesus. A political Jesus suits those who wish to establish religious credentials for their brand of politics. A troubled, sexual Jesus makes for an exciting movie character who showcases existential angst. The image of baby Jesus in a crib evokes family and domesticity, an effective way of attracting Christmas shoppers perhaps, but not a satisfying representation of the man himself.

For that, we have to use the best historical records we have. None of the caricatures stands up if we truly examine what we know about Jesus from history, using all the available sources and giving priority to the most reliable ones. Fortunately for us, the best sources are easily accessible in the pages of the New Testament – in the Gospels known as Matthew, Mark, Luke and John.

When we test these sources against our own cultural ideas, fascinating images of Jesus emerge, some of which we will probably relate to in our own personalities, and some of which will really challenge us about what true humanity should be.

The accurate picture of Jesus is multifaceted, unlike the caricatures. It is a portrait that cannot be painted too quickly. But there are also frustrating gaps in the story of Jesus, gaps left by the random nature of history and the particular records of Jesus that remain from all those centuries ago.

There is a temptation to "fill in the gaps" of Jesus' life – as we will see in the next chapter – but to do so is to move away from the real Jesus and start fabricating one of your own liking. This is entertaining, but ultimately dishonouring and distracting. When so much can be known from history about the man behind the Christian faith, it is surely our responsibility to be careful to paint the most accurate and realistic portrait of him that we possibly can. And, according to the Gospels, one idea more than all others summarizes who he claimed to be: he is *ho Christos*, the Messiah, the one anointed with God's authority not to conquer and overthrow his enemies but to renew them through his love.

CHAPTER 6

BETWEEN GALILEE AND TIBET

THE REAL ACTION OF THE JESUS STORY STARTS NOT DOWN IN Bethlehem in 5 BC in the Christ's humble manger but way up north thirty years later in Jesus' home district of Galilee. Here, this claimed Messiah would announce his message of the kingdom, a message of grace, meekness and non-violence, to all who would listen.

Sceptics of religion have sometimes argued that Jesus invented his hope for the "kingdom come" as a way of coping with the misery of his desert origins in Galilee. Who wouldn't fantasise about the glories of the spiritual realm if you had to put up with the deserts of Galilee? One such critic is French philosopher Michel Onfray, who writes on the opening page of his provocative *The Atheist Manifesto*:

> I thought of the lands of Israel, Judaea and Samaria, of Jerusalem and Bethlehem, of Nazareth and the Sea of Galilee. Places where the sun bakes men's heads, desiccates their bodies, afflicts their souls with thirst. Places that generate

View from a boat on Lake Galilee

a yearning for oases where water flows cool, clear and free, where the air is balmy and fragrant, where food and drink are abundant. The afterlife suddenly struck me as a counter-world invented by men exhausted and parched by their cease-less wanderings across the dunes or up and down rocky trails baked to white heat. Monotheism was born of the sand.[1]

Had Onfray actually visited Nazareth and Galilee he might have written something very different. Jesus' stomping ground was (and is) both beautiful and fertile, serviced by excellent soil and an enormous inland sea known as Lake Galilee. The first-century Jewish writer Josephus, whom I quoted earlier, was a one-time resident of Sepphoris, five miles from Jesus' hometown of Nazareth. He writes of the region:

> For the land is everywhere so rich in soil and pasturage and produces such a variety of trees, that even the most indo-lent are tempted by these facilities to devote themselves to agriculture. In fact, every inch of the soil has been cultivated by the inhabitants; there is not a parcel of waste land. The towns, too, are thickly distributed, and even the villages, thanks to the fertility of the soil, are all so densely populated that the smallest of them contains above fifteen thousand inhabitants.[2]

THE MYTH OF JESUS' EASTERN PILGRIMAGE

But what did Jesus do in Galilee from childhood to his thirties, when he launched his public ministry proclaiming the arrival of God's kingdom? This is a topic of great speculation, including claims that Jesus traveled to faraway lands to learn the philosophy and ethics of the East.

The story of Jesus' pilgrimage to the East originates with the Russian journalist Nicholas Notovitch, who in 1894 claimed to have found a document in a Tibetan monastery that described Jesus' journey to India to learn Hinduism and then on to Tibet to learn Buddhism. From there Jesus apparently returned to Pales-tine to preach his unique wisdom.[3] This was an excellent attempt at East-West fusion, but the whole thing was a hoax. Shortly after these claims emerged, the head abbot of the very monastery Noto-vitch claimed to have visited insisted that no Russian gentleman had come to the community in living memory and that no such document ever existed.

Not only is there a total dearth of evidence for any visit to India and Tibet, it is inherently implausible that any first-century Mediterranean, let alone a marginal Jew from Galilee, made it all the way to Tibet. And other problems exist (historians will be wondering why I am even gracing the theory with a reply). First, there are the obvious contradictions between Eastern philosophy and the teachings of Jesus.[4] Jesus clearly taught that we have just one existence in this world in which we are obliged to worship a personal Creator God who, at the climax of history, will raise the dead *bodily* and renew the physical cosmos itself. All of this is anathema to the great Hindu teachers and the Buddha. If Jesus did travel to India and Tibet, he obviously returned to Palestine having rejected what he learnt there.

The story of Jesus' Eastern pilgrimage nonetheless makes its way into contemporary works. It is found in a book by actress Shirley MacLaine and a TV documentary titled *The Lost Years of Jesus*.[5] The reality is, the theory has about as much going for it as the assertion that the 1969 lunar landing was a NASA fraud filmed in a Hollywood studio. This theory too found its way into a documentary aired on Fox in 2001.[6]

SUPERBOY JESUS

Modern writers are not the only ones who have speculated about the "lost years" of Jesus. Dissatisfied with the silence of the New Testament, an unknown Christian author in the following century produced his own set of stories about the adventures of the child Messiah. The so-called *Infancy Story of Thomas* (not to be confused with the Gnostic *Gospel of Thomas*[7]) is a late-second-century work (around AD 180) that purports to tell "all the works of the childhood of our Lord Jesus Christ and his mighty deeds."[8] The child is a veritable Superboy:

> He made soft clay and fashioned from it twelve sparrows. And it was the Sabbath when he did this. And there were also many other children playing with him. Now when a certain Jew saw what Jesus was doing in his play on the Sabbath, he at once went and told his father Joseph: "See, your child is at

the brook, and he has taken clay and fashioned twelve birds and has profaned the Sabbath." And when Joseph came to the place and saw it, he cried out to him, saying: "Why do you do on the Sabbath what ought not to be done?" But Jesus clapped his hands and cried to the sparrows: "Off with you!" And the sparrows took flight and went away chirping.[9]

Other childhood miracles in the text include raising a friend to life after he accidentally fell off a roof, separating the water of a brook into little ponds and lengthening a piece of wood to even out a bed crafted by his carpenter father. All rather innocent, if fanciful. But on occasion the boy is a bad-tempered superhero:

After this again [Jesus] went through the village, and a lad ran and knocked against his shoulder. Jesus was exasperated and said to him: "You shall not go further on your way," and the child immediately fell down and died.[10]

When the parents of the dead child complained to Joseph — who wouldn't! — the boy Jesus responded by striking his accusers blind.[11] Nice! No one takes these stories seriously, not only because they are so far-fetched but because the *Infancy Story of Thomas* was written too long after Jesus (about 150 years) to hold any possibility of preserving accurate information about him. These are (im-)pious fictions, inventions of a man or group dissatisfied with the Gospels' silence about the childhood of Jesus.

Personally, I am astonished that anyone who claimed to be a follower of Jesus could have produced such stories—a person who relishes the thought of Jesus striking a child dead (for inadvertently bumping into him) has lost his moral, let alone Christian, compass. The Jesus who features here does not at all sound like the one who grew up to insist: "If someone strikes you on the cheek, offer him the other cheek as well."[12] Like the Gnostic Gospels, the *Infancy Story of Thomas* is read for what it tells us about certain second- and third-century splinter groups within Christianity, not for what it reveals about the Jesus of history.

The reality is, like so many other great figures of antiquity whose "glory years" are all we know of them, the Jesus we reliably know about is the *adult* Jesus. There are missing years, for sure, but there is nothing mysterious about them.

JESUS AT TWELVE

All this speculation – both modern and ancient – about Jesus' missing years stands in marked contrast to the disciplined silence of the New Testament about what Jesus did between 5 BC and AD 28. Only one story from that period survives, tucked away in the Gospel of Luke. It is striking in both its brevity and understatement; no dazzling superhero appears here.

Our passage tells how Jesus' family joined the annual pilgrimage to the Jerusalem temple for the great Passover festival, that most holy celebration of Israel's deliverance from Egypt centuries before. As the tour party began to return home after the week-long festivities, Mary and Joseph realized that their twelve-year-old was missing:

> They thought that he was somewhere in their group, and
> they had gone a day's journey before they started to look
> for him among their relatives and friends. Finding noth-
> ing, they returned to Jerusalem to search for him. After
> three days, they found him in the temple, sitting among the
> teachers, listening to them and asking questions. All those
> who heard him were astonished at his level of understand-
> ing, and his answers. When they saw him there, his parents
> were astonished and his mother said to him, "Son, why did
> you treat us like this? Look, your father and I have been
> anxiously searching for you." He said to them, "Why did
> you have to search for me? Didn't you realise that I must be
> in my father's house?" But they didn't understand what he
> was saying to them. Then Jesus went back with his parents
> to Nazareth, and was obedient to them. And his mother
> treasured all these things in her heart (Luke 2:44–51).

The paragraph raises lots of questions for the modern reader: How could Mary and Joseph have started out for Galilee without checking that their eldest son was with them? How could they have travelled a whole day without noticing he was missing? And where did the boy sleep during those few nights alone in Jerusalem? The questions lose some of their force when we try to think in ancient terms rather than modern. A large family travelling with literally hundreds of other pilgrim relatives and friends from the same district could be forgiven for assuming that their eldest was somewhere "in their group." David Flusser, the great Jewish professor of history and religion from the Hebrew University of Jerusalem, notes that "in those days a boy of twelve could be regarded as grown up."[13]

In any case, it is to the Gospel writers' great credit that they showed remarkable restraint in their treatment of the missing years of Jesus. They refused to add exotic tales of boyhood powers or travels to distant lands, even though they believed him to be the Christ, the one anointed to speak and act for God. All we have is a single story about Jesus' early precociousness.

As boring as it sounds for one destined to found the world's largest religion, Jesus almost certainly spent his youth simply working in his father's business of carpentry, making chests, locks, doors, furniture, ploughs and houses.[14] In other words, the majority of Jesus' life was spent in relative obscurity, with no apparent hint of his future significance as the Christian Messiah. It fits rather well with Jesus' humble beginnings as told by Luke. What else would we expect from one laid in a manger at birth?

CHAPTER 7

THE FIRST TEMPTATION OF CHRIST

WHEN JESUS FINALLY DID GO PUBLIC WITH HIS WORLD-CHANGING message it was not in a cosmopolitan city like Sepphoris or a religious capital like Jerusalem. It was out by the Jordan River where another prophet-like figure was already preaching.

Away from the power-centre of Jerusalem, one of first-century Judaism's most significant figures was causing a stir – John the Baptist:

> John went throughout the country around the Jordan, proclaiming a baptism of repentance for the forgiveness of sins.... John said to the crowds that had come out to be baptised by him, "You snakes! Who warned you to flee

Ritual bath at Qumran

from the coming wrath? … Indeed, the axe is already poised at the root of the trees; and every tree that does not produce good fruit is cut down and thrown into the fire." … The expectations of the people began to rise, and everyone wondered in their hearts whether he might not be the Christ. In answer to this, John said to all of them, "I baptise you with water; but someone much stronger than me is coming—I would not even be worthy to undo the strap of his sandal. He will baptise you with the Holy Spirit and fire" (Luke 3:3–16).

John is not just a strange character at the start of the Gospel story but an important figure in Palestine in his own right. The first-century Jewish writer Josephus confirms that great crowds of people were mesmerised by his preaching and flocked to him for baptism.[1] Baptism (meaning "to dip") was a Jewish ritual symbolising cleansing before God; it was a spiritual bath. The Essenes of Qumran–the Jewish sect that gave us the Dead Sea Scrolls–practised similar "dippings" in purpose-built ritual baths called *mikvaot*. These washings were a daily reminder of the contaminations of the world and the need for divine cleansing.

John intensified the meaning. He announced a grand new era in God's dealings with the world. He called people to a decisive moment of repentance, or turning back to God. What was needed therefore was not daily washing but one powerful moment of surrender to God, a moment of cleansing and renewal. And so was born the one-off baptism.

Jesus publicly submitted to John's defining ritual. That is really interesting. It may be too much to say that Jesus was a disciple of John, as some scholars have suggested,[2] but of all the Jewish teachers active in Palestine in the period, it does seem that the Baptist was the one he most admired and identified with as something of a mentor.[3] Certainly, the theme of a grand moment of renewal and forgiveness would mark the entire ministry of Jesus. Going out to the Jordan River, rather than going public in Sepphoris or Jerusalem, tells us that Jesus' concerns were less to do with politics and power and more to do with the deeper issues of the human heart. In his mind, the role of the Messiah was not to conquer but to renew and redeem.

DECISION OF A LIFETIME

But, first, Jesus would embark on a significant journey into the wilderness of Judea (where, in contrast with Galilee, there really are deserts). Here he would face the decision of a lifetime: would he opt for the path of power over Israel's enemies, the path expected of the Christ, or would he walk the road of humility? Three of the Gospels tell us that, after his baptism, Jesus experienced some kind of spiritual trial—a visionary battle with the dark side. And at least one of the temptations had to do with the quest for power and glory.

> Then the Devil led him up high and showed him all the kingdoms of the world in a moment of time. And the Devil said to him, "I will give all this authority to you, and the glory of all these kingdoms, because it is mine to give. And I can give it to anyone I wish. If, then, you will worship me, all of it will be yours." But Jesus replied to him, "It is written, 'You are to worship the Lord your God, and serve him alone.'" ... And when the Devil had finished every test, he left Jesus until an opportune time. Jesus returned in the power of the Spirit to Galilee, and a report about him spread throughout the whole region. He taught in their synagogues, and everybody spoke glowingly of him (Luke 4:1–16).

The text is interesting in terms of our understanding of Jesus as Messiah. "I'll give you all the kingdoms of the world," said the dark voice in Jesus' desert vision, "if you just worship me." This was Jesus' moment of decision: a choice between the way of domination and the path of humble service of God and people. Jesus obviously chose the latter. For him, God's kingdom was revealed not through strength and violence but through his own teaching, healings and, ultimately, self-sacrifice. What his humble birth hinted at, his teaching and life course would exemplify. This wilderness temptation was the moment he resolutely turned his back on the expected *military* Messiah who would gain possession of all the kingdoms of the world. Ever since then, true Christianity follows Jesus in shunning the temptation to power and violence.

DOESN'T RELIGION PURSUE
POWER AND VIOLENCE?

This is probably the point to raise a question you might have been pondering over the last few pages. Sure, Jesus endorsed the path of peace and nonretaliation, but hasn't the Christian church sometimes acted very differently?

The complaint that religion leads to violence has been in the *Top 10 Reasons Not to Be a Christian* for decades, but in the last few years it has gone to about No. 3 with a bullet. At lunch a few months ago, a friend of a friend insisted with complete sincerity that Christianity had caused "most of the wars of history." I asked him to be specific and he mentioned the Crusades, the Spanish Inquisition and Northern Ireland—not exactly "most wars," but for him these were powerful icons of the violence and imperialism of the church. Perhaps the most articulate statement of the complaint has been made by Christopher Hitchens in his aptly titled *God Is Not Great: How Religion Poisons Everything*:

> We believe with certainty that an ethical life can be lived without religion. And we know for a fact that the corollary holds true—that religion has caused innumerable people not just to conduct themselves no better than others, but to award themselves permission to behave in ways that would make a brothel-keeper or an ethnic cleanser to raise an eyebrow.[4] ...
>
> In Belfast I have seen whole streets burned out by sectarian warfare between different sects of Christianity, and interviewed people whose relatives and friends have been kidnapped and killed or tortured by rival religious death squads, often for no other reason than membership of another confession.[5]

Hitchens and the others are surely right, at least in part. Christians have done and said abominable things in the name of Christ. This is not just a Roman Catholic problem, with their much-publicized Crusades and Inquisitions. Protestants have their own dark history. Martin Luther, the German founder of the Protestant movement, wrote the most despicable things about European Jews in his 1543 booklet "The Jews and Their Lies." John Calvin, the leading voice of the Reformed tradition and one of my favourite theologians, was brutal in his treatment of heretics like Michael Servetus, who was executed in 1553 for unorthodox views about the Trinity.[6] These are terrible departures from the ethos of Jesus by sincere Christians. Modern believers ought to face them and admit that the church has frequently failed to live up to Christ's standards.

WHERE CRITICS GO WRONG

This is not to say that critics like Hitchens are entirely right. First, it has to be said that modern retellings of the misdeeds of the church frequently involve gross exaggerations. In his recent book *Atheist Delusions,* Prof David Bentley Hart points out that every new era tends to retell the past in a way that elevates its own position as the great deliverer and bringer of special freedoms, and demotes the reputation of the previous generation. This necessarily requires exaggerating, even lying, about the horrors of the past. We do this on a small scale when we talk about the moralism of the 1950s or the prudishness of Victorian England. It happened on a macro scale in the eighteenth–nineteenth centuries, argues Hart, when Enlightenment leaders popularised the expression "Dark Ages." Here was an attempt to describe the era of Christendom as a time of oppression, ignorance and violence, overcome by the era of freedom and peace brought about by secular reason. However, as Hart points out, this is little more than "a simple and enchanting tale, easily followed and utterly captivating in its explanatory tidiness; its sole defect is that it happens to be false in every identifiable detail. This tale of the birth of the modern world has largely disappeared from respectable academic literature."[7]

Let me offer two examples of these exaggerated retellings of the past. The Spanish Inquisition is often thought to be Christianity at its most bloodthirsty with hundreds of thousands of heretics killed (trawl the Internet and you will even find estimates of a million or more). However, in its 350-year history, the Spanish Inquisition probably killed around 6,000 people.[8] That comes out at eighteen deaths a year. Of course, one a year – one ever – is too much, but the figure hardly sustains the monstrous narratives we often hear. Or take the iconic Northern Ireland conflict. The thirty-year "troubles" led to the deaths of fewer than 4,000 people. Again, one death "in the name of Christ" is a blasphemy, but how did the Northern Ireland conflict ever come to symbolize the ferocity of the church? Compare it with the thoroughly secular French Revolution. As many people were executed in the name of "liberty, equality and fraternity" in a single year of the Revolution (the "Terror" of September 1793–July 1794) as were killed in the entire three decades of the "troubles."[9] And I am still in favour of liberty, equality and fraternity.

And this is my second problem with the complaint of Hitchens and others. The violence of Christendom is dwarfed by that of non-religious causes, such as World War I (8,000,000 deaths) and World War II (35,000,000 deaths). Then there is the very awkward fact that the twentieth century's three great atheistic regimes were hotbeds of unrestrained violence. Joseph Stalin's openly atheistic project killed at least 20,000,000 people, which is more people each week than the Spanish Inquisition killed in its entire 350-year history. Pol Pot, another avowed atheist, is known to have slaughtered 2,000,000 people out of a population of 8,000,000. I must emphasise that this is not to claim that atheists are more violent than Christians. It simply underlines that violence is a perennial *human* problem, not a specifically religious one. And those like Christopher Hitchens who suggest that these communist regimes were quasi-religious in their zeal and so provide further evidence of the pernicious effect of religion have abandoned sincere investigation into the problem and settled upon crass anti-religious apologetics. Better to state the obvious: religion or irreligion can inspire hatred.

The claim that religion has started most of the wars of history ought to cause embarrassment to thinking people. And yet it remains, as David Bentley Hart points out, "the sort of remark that sets many heads sagely nodding in recognition of what seems an undeniable truth. Such sentiments have become so much a part of the conventional grammar of 'enlightened' scepticism that they are scarcely ever subjected to serious scrutiny."[10]

At best, the criticisms of Hitchens and others prove only that Christians have not been Christian enough (sincere believers confess that daily). For anyone can tell you that when Christians are violent and imperialistic they are not obeying their Messiah but defying him who said "love your enemy and do good to those who hate you." The solution to religious violence, then, is not less Christianity but more. As the brilliant Yale University philosopher-theologian Prof Miroslav Volf writes:

When it comes to Christianity the cure against religiously induced and legitimized violence is almost exactly the opposite of what an important intellectual current in the West since the Enlightenment has been suggesting. The cure is not less religion, but, in a carefully qualified sense, more religion.... The more the Christian faith matters to its adherents as faith and the more they practice it as an ongoing tradition with strong ties to its origins and with clear cognitive and moral content, the better off we will be.[11]

The same point was made years ago by our deist friend Albert Einstein. Though a Jew and painfully aware of the inconsistencies of the German church, he believed that what Germany needed in that crucial hour was not less Christianity but more. In his 1915 essay "My Opinion of the War" he wrote: "But why so many words when I can say it in one sentence, and in a sentence very appropriate for a Jew. Honour your master, Jesus Christ, not only in words and songs but, rather, foremost in your deeds."[12] The solution to violent Christianity is real Christianity.

Finally, there is an awkward question that atheist critics ought to face. It has to do with atheism's intellectual capacity to restrain hatred and inspire love. Christians and atheists alike are capable of both love and hate. Agreed. But when Christians love, they do so in full accordance with their worldview that begins with the love of God and the inherent value of his much-loved creatures. When Christians hate, they do so in logical defiance of that worldview. But here is the question: what is there in the atheist's perspective that can rationally inspire love and discourage hate? I know that most atheists (in the Christianized West) choose love over hate. That is to be applauded. But if human beings are accidents in an unknowing universe, how can the decision to love or hate be anything more than a preference, a product of "feelings," as atheist Bertrand Russell once famously acknowledged? On what grounds can the atheist speak rationally of the high and equal value of the poor or the weak or the asylum seeker? Put another way, while it is obvious that only one way of life is logically compatible with Christianity (the Messiah's way of humility and love), any kind of life is logically compatible with atheism.

PART 3

KINGDOM COME

Jesus' Vision of the Future
and Its Relevance Now

CHAPTER 8

A TEACHER AMONG TEACHERS

I WAS ONCE INTERVIEWED ON AUSTRALIAN RADIO ABOUT THE PERson of Jesus—not such a common thing on our secular stations. I was happy enough with how it went, but I braced myself when the announcer opened the phone lines for comment from listeners. To my surprise, while most callers had negative things to say about Christians or the church, every caller heaped praise on Jesus himself. They loved his ethics, his example, his critique of religion and his general approach to life and faith. In their view, he was the ultimate guru-figure, a teacher among teachers. It is probably fair to say that Jesus' teaching is the most famous aspect of his ministry. We don't quite know what to make of his healings or his death and resurrection, but his *words* still resonate all these years later. Some have become proverbial in the English language: "the blind leading the blind," "turn the other cheek," "salt of the earth," "seek and you will find" and many others. But to truly understand Jesus as a teacher we need to set him in the context of the many other teachers of his period. Then we will see how

John Dickson at the Shrine of the Book in Jerusalem with the *Rule of the Community* from the Dead Sea Scrolls

truly remarkable he was, and how appropriate it is that even the most sceptical Westerner today reveres the wisdom of the man from Nazareth.

GRAECO-ROMAN TEACHERS

The ancient world was famous for its philosopher-teachers and for the "schools" or groups of disciples they established.[1] Pythagoras in the late sixth century BC gathered students together and taught them a range of esoteric doctrines and a way of life that included wearing white linen, obeying certain dietary rules and sharing possessions. Curiously, at their initiation disciples were required to swear an oath never to reveal the Pythagorean teachings to non-members. Pythagoras was also famous for mathematical discoveries and the analysis of musical-harmony theory.[2]

In the fifth century BC, Protagoras—a teacher of grammar, literature and philosophy known as a Sophist—rose to prominence. People would pay large fees to hear him speak. It was said that he could argue any side of a case and, if he wanted to, he could make the weakest arguments sound the strongest. He is also the first known relativist, arguing that each person's 'truth' depends entirely on his or her perspective: "Man is the measure of all things," he said; "Things are for every man what they seem to him to be."[3] Some of these ideas still flourish today.

But not everyone agreed. In the following century Plato (428–348 BC), whose name is virtually synonymous with philosophy, critiqued Protagoras. He pointed out that if things are for each person what they simply seem to him to be, then even Protagoras' theory is relative and therefore not true in any substantial sense. Hard to argue with, really. Plato founded an academy in Athens for the pursuit of ethical, spiritual and physical truth that lasted until AD 529. It was the ancient world's Oxford University, which is also about 900 years old (though Oxford shows no signs of closing down anytime soon).

Other ancient teachers with disciples included Epicurus of Athens (341–270 BC) who taught that "pleasure is the beginning and end of living happily."[4] Of course, from him comes the modern description of pleasure-seekers as "epicureans." Then there is Zeno (335–263 BC), the founder of Stoicism, a popular philosophy among the intelligentsia. He argued that happiness is found in strict mental and emotional discipline; hence, the contemporary tag "stoic."

A more extreme form of stoicism was practised by the Cynics, a group of austere philosopher-preachers led by Diogenes in the fourth century BC, who lived outdoors, dressed in simple robes and scavenged or begged for food. It was probably this rough lifestyle that earned them the name Cynics, from the Greek word *kunikos* or "dog-like." The Cynics lasted well beyond the time of Jesus, and it has even been suggested that Jesus himself was part of the movement. But, as Graham Stanton has pointed out, "Those who portray Jesus primarily or solely as a wisdom teacher or Jewish Cynic have built dubious hypothesis upon dubious hypothesis.[5]

JEWISH TEACHERS

More important for understanding Jesus as a teacher are the many Jewish rabbis living in Palestine in this period.[6] The Gospels speak regularly of Jesus' encounters, usually clashes, with anonymous "teachers of the law." But numerous other texts in our possession put names to these intellectuals. One of them in fact shared Jesus' name – Yeshua ben Sira (Jesus, son of Sira) – who wrote what is called the *Wisdom of Ben Sira* (or *Ecclesiasticus*) in Jerusalem in 132 BC. Throughout his teaching he insists that true wisdom is found in the Jewish tradition not in the philosophy of the Greeks, which by this time had become all-pervasive. Mind you, some of what this Jesus taught might surprise modern readers, such as the following collection of advice about eating and drinking at banquets (which I have stuck on my fridge door at home!):

How ample a little is for a well-disciplined person! He does not breathe heavily when in bed.

Healthy sleep depends on moderate eating; he rises early, and feels fit. The distress of sleeplessness and of nausea and colic are with the glutton.

If you are overstuffed with food, get up to vomit, and you will have relief.

Wine drunk at the proper time and in moderation is rejoicing of heart and gladness of soul. Wine drunk to excess leads to bitterness of spirit, to quarrels and stumbling.

Speak, you who are older, for it is your right, but with accurate knowledge, and do not interrupt the music. Where there is entertainment, do not pour out talk; do not display your cleverness at the wrong time.

A ruby seal in a setting of gold is a concert of music at a banquet of wine. A seal of emerald in a rich setting of gold is the melody of music with good wine.[7]

Two of the most famous Jewish teachers of the period were Rabbis Shammai and Hillel. In fact, these two are credited with founding the two great "schools" of ancient Judaism. A delightful story is told in the Talmud, a Jewish law book, that highlights the rigidness of Shammai and the flexibility of Hillel. A non-Jew (Gentile) approaches both teachers and asks if it is possible to become a convert to Judaism speedily. The differing answers are revealing:

> On another occasion it happened that a certain heathen came before Shammai and said to him, "Make me a proselyte on condition that you teach me the whole Torah while I stand on one foot." Shammai drove him out with the builder's cubit which was in his hand. When he went before Hillel, he made him a proselyte. He said to him, "What is hateful to you, do not do to your neighbor. That is the whole Torah. The rest is commentary. Go and learn."[8]

Careful readers will notice the similarity between Hillel's "What is hateful to you, do not do to your neighbor" and the so-called Golden Rule of Jesus in the Gospel of Luke: "In the way you want people to treat you, do the same for them" or in its traditional form "Do to others as you would have them do to you."[9] Some have argued that there is little difference between Hillel's formulation (refrain from the wrong you don't want done to yourself) and Jesus' positive version (do the good that you want others to do to you). They point out that this Golden Rule appears also in pre-Christian Greek and Chinese traditions, such as this one from Confucius: "Do not inflict on others what you yourself would not wish done to you."[10] But is there really no difference between *avoiding doing harm to others* and *actively doing good to them?* Perhaps it is my Christian bias, but the two ideas make quite different demands on us. Jesus asked for much more than simply not hurting other people; he insisted that we seek for others the good we would like them to do for us. It seems Jesus took a generally accepted axiom about reciprocity and intensified it in the direction of love. He took a common Silver Rule, you could say, and refined it into the Golden Rule.

THE KINGDOM COME

Jesus was far more than a wandering philosopher handing out proverbs about doing good. Much of what he said was far more confronting – for ancients and moderns.

Scholars agree that nothing was more central to Jesus' message than the "kingdom of God."[11] Luke records him telling people, "I must proclaim the good news of the kingdom because that is why I was sent" (Luke 4:43). In the famous Lord's Prayer, he urged people to pray "Your kingdom come ..." (Luke 11:2).

The kingdom of God was a very Jewish idea. From the Old Testament to the Dead Sea Scrolls, Jews talked about a day when the Creator would prove himself "King" over the world, when he would overthrow injustice and restore order to this hurtful and chaotic planet. The biblical Psalm 145:11 – 12 declares, "They tell of the glory of your kingdom and speak of your might, so that all people may know of your mighty acts and the glorious splendor of your kingdom." The Essenes, the guardians of the Dead Sea Scrolls, were especially interested in the kingdom, so much so that they removed themselves from Jerusalem a century or more before Jesus and set up an alternative community in the desert of Qumran. They believed the holy city had become corrupt and they fully expected it to be judged when the kingdom came: "His realm is above the powerful mighty, and before the might of his power all are terrified and scatter; they flee before the radiance of his glorious kingdom."[12] Those of us who have ever wished the Almighty would do something about the mess in the world have wished for what ancient Jews called the kingdom of God.

The kingdom of God was connected with the arrival of the Messiah – the king in this kingdom – who would sweep away oppressors and establish a new world order of justice and peace. This is precisely the perspective of the Pharisee who wrote the previously mentioned *Psalms of Solomon* shortly after the Romans arrived in Jerusalem in 63 BC: "the kingdom of God is forever over the nations in judgement. Lord, you chose David to be king over Israel, and swore to him about his descendants forever, that his kingdom should not fail."[13]

The desire to throw off the shackles of Rome and establish God's kingdom had been brewing for decades. In 4 BC Judah son of Hezekiah led a rebellion in Sepphoris, near Jesus' home-town of Nazareth.[14] Ten years later Judas the Galilean urged his compatriots to resist a Roman census with violence. His battle cry was "No ruler but God."[15] Things reached their climax in the year AD 66 when total war broke out – with devastating consequences. One by one, Jewish towns were crushed. At Gamla, a town of Galilee built into the side of a steep mountain, the residents must have thought they could beat the Romans. They started to mint coins heralding a new era for God's people; the inscription reads: "For the redemption of Jerusalem." The kingdom of God seemed within reach. But like Jerusalem a few years later, valiant Gamla was overcome in November AD 67. Arrowheads and catapults recovered from the site indicate something of the ferocity of the month-long siege. According to Josephus, when the Romans eventually took Gamla, "on all sides was heard the never ending moan of the dying, and the whole city was deluged with blood pouring down the slopes."[16] Enraged after so long a siege, the Romans even took to throwing infants from the citadel. Despairing of hope, thousands of Jews "plunged headlong with their wives and children into the ravine," said Josephus.[17] All hopes for a victorious Messiah and a glorious kingdom were dashed.

I hardly need to point out that Jesus saw the kingdom of God arriving very differently. For him, the kingdom would not come as a tornado of judgement on the ungodly. It would start small, almost unnoticed. On one occasion he likened God's kingdom to a mustard seed, one of the smallest known at the time:

> What is the kingdom of God like and to what shall I compare it? It is like a mustard seed that someone took and threw into his garden. It grew and became a tree, and the birds of the air nested in its branches (Luke 13:18–19).

The kingdom of God would appear in a most unexpected way.

KINGDOM OF LOVE

Perhaps the most unusual part of Jesus' teaching about the kingdom was his insistence that the citizens of this new era were to be marked, above all, by love – even the love of enemies:

> Love your enemies. Do good to those who hate you.
> Bless those who curse you. Pray for those who mistreat you.
> If someone strikes you on the cheek, offer him the other
> cheek as well.... And in the way you want people to treat
> you, do the same for them.... Be merciful, as your Father is
> merciful (Luke 6:27–29, 31, 36).

Jesus wasn't the first to speak about love – it had a long tradition going back to the Jewish Scriptures. But he did intensify the idea and apply it in quite a radical way.

In Jesus' first-century context, the command to love your enemy meant more than just being nice to the annoying neighbour over the back fence – though that's not a bad place to start – it meant doing good to those who would conquer you. And it is just as radical today. Recently, just north of Jesus' Galilee, there was a brief war between Israeli forces and Hezbollah fighters up in Lebanon. Imagine asking both sides to turn the other cheek and love each other. For Jesus, the kingdom of God was a kingdom of love, and those who belonged to that kingdom were to love as God loves.

The contrast with the teaching of the Dead Sea Scrolls (written shortly before Jesus) could hardly be more dramatic. In the opening paragraph of the famous *Rule of the Community*, which sets out the fundamentals of life among the Essenes, we find the following statement of the purpose of this radical Jewish community:

> in order to be united in the counsel of God and walk in
> perfection in his sight, complying with all revealed things
> concerning the regulated times of their stipulations; in order
> to love all the sons of light, each one according to his lot in
> God's plan, and to detest all the sons of darkness, each one in
> accordance with his guilt.[18]

If one was to love the neighbour, it made sense to the Essenes that one should hate the enemy; it was a logic Jesus repudiated. Although other Jewish groups advocated the importance of love,

Jesus did apparently go further than ever before, as the Jewish scholar David Flusser remarked:

> In the clear purity of his love they must have detected something very special. Jesus did not accept all that was thought and taught in the Judaism of his time. Although not really a Pharisee himself, he was closest to the Pharisees of the school of Hillel, who preached love, but he pointed the way further to unconditional love—even of one's enemies and of sinners. This was no sentimental doctrine.[19]

At the heart of Jesus' teaching was the promise of the kingdom of God. But at the heart of the kingdom—for Jesus, if not for all of his contemporaries—was the triumph of love not victory over enemies.

JESUS DID NOT JUST *TEACH* ABOUT THE KINGDOM OF GOD. According to all the sources, including those written by non-Christians, Jesus demonstrated the kingdom in what believers call miracles.

But what can the historian say about reports of Jesus healing the sick, giving sight to the blind, calming wild storms and so on? More than you might think.

For one thing, we know that news of a successful healer would have spread like wildfire. And for this we have some very intimate evidence. Marian was a local Jewish woman in Galilee whose daughter, Ya'itha, was struck down by a terrible fever; in the ancient world this was often a death sentence. Marian went to a Jewish holy man and asked for a special blessing. The sage prepared an amulet, a kind of good-luck charm, with special words expertly written out. These were to be said repeatedly over Ya'itha in the hope God would heal her. Marian could never have imagined that centuries later we would find her amulet on the

Synagogue in
Capernaum

eastern side of Lake Galilee. We catch a glimpse here into the real-life terror of illness in the ancient world and of a parent's longing for the welfare of a child. The words read:

> A good amulet to heal Ya'itha the daughter of Marian from the fever and the shiver and the Evil Eye. Abrasax Ya Y a Yahu El El El QQQQQQQQQQ SSSSSS.... In the name of I-am-who-I-am Amen Amen Selah. A good amulet to drive out the fever and the shiver and the hectic (fever) from Ya'itha the daughter of Marian. In the name of Kariel, Kasiel, Zariel SSSSSS in the name of QQQQQQQQQQQQ....[1]

The strange repetition of nonsensical words and letters here was part of a widespread belief at the time that specially crafted incantations could win the favour of the Almighty.

The contrast with Jesus could hardly be greater. Instead of complicated prayers and blessed trinkets, Jesus, according to the Gospels, simply spoke and people were healed. On one occasion as Jesus was preaching in the synagogue in Capernaum, a man said to be demon possessed screams out, "What do you want with us, Jesus of Nazareth? Have you come to destroy us?" Jesus simply says "Be quiet," and the man falls down, instantly in his right mind (Luke 4:33–35). No rituals, no amulets–just a word.

Jesus leaves the synagogue and goes to the home of Peter, one of his key disciples. Peter's mother-in-law is sick in bed with the dreaded fever. Jesus speaks a word and she is immediately well. In fact, the texts say she gets up and makes dinner for everyone (Luke 4:38–39)–no rest for women in the ancient world. By sundown a virtual doctor's waiting room has sprung up right in the middle of Capernaum. The whole town is at the door with its sick. With a word or a touch, we're told, Jesus heals them all (Luke 4:40).

MIRACLES AND HISTORY

Stories like these seem the stuff of legend not historical reporting. The problem is, we have statements about Jesus' healing capabilities from seven independent sources written within a generation of his life.[2] In ancient history, this is excellent evidence. In addition to the Christian evidence (which, remember, historians neither privilege nor dismiss), we have the first-century Jewish writer,

Josephus, who describes Jesus as "one who wrought surprising feats."[3] The expression "surprising feats" translates the Greek *paradoxa erga*, literally "baffling deeds." It is the Jewish historian's hesitant, non-committal way of relating Jesus' widespread fame as a miracle-worker. Geza Vermes, the famous Jewish professor from Oxford University, is right when he says, "For Christians Jesus was the miracle working Son of God. For later, hostile Jews he was a magician. Josephus stands in the middle: for him Jesus was a wise man and a performer of extraordinary deeds."[4] There can be little doubt, in other words, that friend and foe alike thought Jesus to be a wonder-worker of some kind. Two later non-Christian passages also refer to Jesus' miracles, albeit in a highly negative way. The Greek intellectual Celsus dismisses the reports as Egyptian magic (*Contra Celsum* 1.28, 68) and the ancient Jewish law book, the Talmud, condemns Jesus for practising "sorcery" (*b. Sanhedrin* 43a). James Dunn of Durham University notes: "What is interesting in this testimony, hardly partisan on behalf of Christian claims, is that the accounts of Jesus' healing and exorcistic success are nowhere disputed, only the reasons for that success."[5]

Compare this evidence with that of another healer from the first century, who is often put forward by sceptics as a parallel to Jesus. Born in the city of Tyana in eastern Turkey, Apollonius was said to have travelled widely throughout the Mediterranean preaching his Neo-pythagorean philosophy and performing countless wonders, including raising a young girl from death.[6] The problem with the stories about Apollonius, however, is that they come from just one source, *Life of Apollonius*, written by the philosopher Philostratus (AD 172–250) around the year AD 220, 120 years after Apollonius' death. It hardly compares with Jesus. Virtually everyone involved in the academic study of this topic, regardless of his general scepticism about miracles, is happy to conclude that, in the case of Jesus, the evidence establishes beyond doubt that he engaged in activities thought by those around him to be miraculous.[7] This is a conclusion without parallel in the study of ancient history.

MIRACLES AND THE MODERN MIND

Let me clear up a misunderstanding. "Miracle" is probably not the best word for a discussion of Jesus' healings and exorcisms. From the Latin *miraculum*, "object of wonder," in modern discussions the term has come to mean something like *a supernatural contradiction or violation of the laws of nature*. There is an entire worldview locked up in this description, one heavily indebted to the Enlightenment, particularly the eighteenth-century Scottish philosopher David Hume.[8] It assumes a dualism, the presence of two worlds: an observable, physical one, and a hidden, spiritual one. When that spiritual world overrides the physical one, we have a miracle. Of course, philosophical materialists flat out deny any spiritual dimension to existence but their definition of a miracle still involves a hypothetical incursion into the natural world by something extraneous to it. I suspect some religious people today likewise think of miracles in terms of two worlds colliding – God bending or breaking the natural order to achieve some astonishing purpose.

But the Gospel writers did not think in this dualistic way. From their point of view – the Jewish point of view – there are not two worlds at all, just one, and God is its sole Creator and Sustainer. Everything that happens in the universe, from the rising of the sun to the gift of breath itself, is the powerful work of God. Whatever happens in the world, in other words, is *his* action in *his* world. As a result, Jews and Christians thought of miracles not as invasions from a parallel world but as special examples of God's preserving power in his creation.[9]

The difference may seem slight, but in historical study it is important to try to think of things from the viewpoint of those we are studying rather than from our own perspective; how else can we stay attentive to the subtleties in the evidence? In any case, it is from within this Jewish worldview, where the Creator is constantly attending to his creation, that the Gospel writers describe Jesus' baffling deeds not as supernatural or miraculous, but as special examples of *power*. The typical Greek terms in the Gospels are *dunameis*, which means "strength" or "authority," and *sēmeia*, which means "signs."[10] The former describes Jesus as powerfully acting *within* and *for* the created order. The latter indicates that these displays of power pointed beyond themselves to some larger meaning. N. T. Wright, both a noted theologian and historian, says of these Greek terms:

> These words do not carry, as the English word "miracle"
> has sometimes done, overtones of invasion from another

world, or from outer space. They indicate, rather, that something has happened, *within* what we would call the "natural" world, which is not what would have been anticipated, and which seems to provide evidence for the active presence of an authority, a power, a work, not invading the created order as an alien force, but rather enabling it to be more truly itself.[11]

Whether or not we accept miracles today involves a personal, philosophical judgement. The historical evidence is of exactly the kind you would expect if Jesus really did perform healings, but if you do not believe in the possibility of miracles, then that sort of evidence will be meaningless.

If you believe there is a God or gods, it should not be very hard to believe in miracles. After all, a God who created the universe is no stranger to doing miraculous deeds. It is God's world, and he can do as he wishes in it. If you are a theist of any kind, it certainly does make sense to believe that miracles are possible.

This is an important starting point for any discussion of miracles, since it establishes what we consider to be ultimate reality. If ultimate reality is God, and especially if this concept is of a God who is powerful, personal and interested in the world, then the possibility that miracles take place is more than zero, and the probability that miracles occur is enhanced.

If you do not believe there is a God, it is a bigger ask! Ultimate reality for such a person is something else – maybe a set of laws, or nothingness. Whatever way you look at it, the miracles recorded in the Bible are either big lies or deceptions, or major evidence that something fascinating is taking place. The first part of any answer to the miracles question will require answering the question of God's existence to your satisfaction.

Philosophically inclined people often cite David Hume as their authority on why miracles are not worth believing. Hume famously stated: "no testimony is sufficient to establish a miracle, unless the testimony be of such a kind, that its falsehood would be more miraculous than the fact which it endeavours to establish."[12] You might want to read that through a few times (I certainly did when I first came across it). Hume is saying that a miracle can only be established by testimony that is practically impossible to disbelieve – i.e., testimony that is so irrefutable it would be a miracle if it were false. A glance at the philosophical literature will reveal some basic flaws in Hume's dictum.[13] It is a statement designed to *rule out* miracles, not to probe whether they can be rationally accepted.

Consider the following. Imagine if the entire population of the world *bar one* witnessed an apparition in the heavens announcing Richard Dawkins as God's favourite atheist. Would the single individual overlooked by the Almighty be able, on Hume's reasoning, to accept the testimony of everyone around him? The answer is no. Since the falsehood of even *universal* testimony would not necessarily be miraculous, the lone agnostic would be obliged to disbelieve, perhaps reasoning that it was a mass hoax. This ridiculous example highlights the implicit unfairness of Hume's principle. Surely, a dictum so grossly stacked against the acceptance of any and all testimony about miracles should be consigned to the absurd. In the end, Hume and other sceptics reject miracles because they already "know" miracles don't occur. They assume what they claim to demonstrate.

Others have a different take on miracles, equally governed by philosophical assumptions. Many of us look at the laws of nature and find ourselves compelled to think that there is a Mind behind the universe. The reasoning goes like this: a universe that "banged" into existence with sophisticated and elegant laws of physics already in place (as cosmologists remind us was the case) is more likely to be the result of a grand Mind than a big accident. Add to this the fact that this universe has (through these physical laws) eventually produced beings like us, with minds that can grasp these laws, and the "accident" theory seems even less satisfying. In short, many would say that we have just the sort of universe you would expect if there is a Creator behind it and the kind of universe you could never expect if there were not.

This belief in some kind of Creator immediately opens up the possibility that the Creator could perform deeds that are (to us) "miraculous." The only question is whether there is good evidence for such a miracle. The fact that we may have never personally experienced such a display of power would rightly inspire a certain scepticism toward claims of miracles—Hume was right about that—but our assumption about the presence of a Lawgiver behind the laws of nature gives us the freedom to accept a miraculous interpretation of an event, if the evidence points strongly in that direction. The fact that in Jesus we have exactly the kind of evidence we would expect if miracles had taken place makes the Gospel stories about him utterly believable to many.

MIRACLES AND THE KINGDOM COME

There is something else historians are confident about: the *meaning* Jesus attached to his baffling deeds. For Jesus, his healings were not sorcery, trickery or even proofs of power. They were signs that the kingdom of God had arrived.

After one of Jesus' many so-called exorcisms we are told that some were suggesting Jesus' power was not from God but from the dark side. Jesus' reply to this criticism, which is recorded in two separate sources, tells us what he thought his actions were about:

> Every kingdom that is divided against itself comes to ruin; and every house that is against itself falls. If Satan also is divided against himself, how will his kingdom stand? For you say, "By Beelzebul he drives out the demons." However, if it is by the finger of God that I drive out the demons, then surely the kingdom of God now confronts you (Luke 11:17–20).

According to the Old Testament, God's kingdom would overthrow evil and restore health and harmony to the world. That is what Jesus thought was going on when he cast out evil spirits and restored sick bodies: these were signs that "the kingdom of God now confronts you." James Dunn explains further:

> Jesus was remembered not simply as a great exorcist, but also as claiming that his exorcisms demonstrated the fulfilment of hopes long cherished for a final release from the power of evil. If the manifestation of God's final reign was to be marked by the binding of Satan, then Jesus' exorcisms showed, to that extent at least, that the binding of Satan had already happened or was already happening, the final exercise of God's rule was already in effect.[14]

As strange as it sounds today, in his miracles Jesus was offering a *preview* of the kingdom, an advance screening of the time when God will put everything right in this world. He not only taught about the kingdom, he offered a glimpse of it. Another passage points in the same direction.

Sometime during AD 28–29 John the Baptist was arrested, then executed by the tetrarch of Galilee, Herod Antipas. The event is described in both the Gospels and Josephus, as we have seen. Before his death, John apparently learned of his protégé's increasing fame and sent some of his remaining disciples to ask Jesus a crucial question: are you *the one*? The expectation of the kingdom–if not the precise language–is clear in both the question and the answer:

> When John heard in prison what the Messiah was doing,
> he sent his disciples to ask him, "Are you the one who was
> to come, or should we expect someone else?" Jesus replied,
> "Go back and report to John what you hear and see: The
> blind receive sight, the lame walk, those who have leprosy
> are cleansed, the deaf hear, the dead are raised, and the
> good news is proclaimed to the poor. Blessed is anyone who
> does not stumble on account of me" (Matthew 11:2–6;
> Luke 7:18–23).

A bit of biblical and historical background will illuminate this intriguing exchange. As we will soon see, most scholars detect in Jesus' words an announcement of the end of one era in human history and the beginning of another. Let me explain.

Many Jews in this period understood themselves to be living under the divine curses foretold centuries earlier in the fifth book of their Scriptures called Deuteronomy. In Deuteronomy 28 we find a long list of punishments that would be meted out to Israel if the nation turned away from worshipping the one true God. These would include fever, skin disease, blindness, insanity and a number of other unpleasant physical conditions, like death.[15]

Later, the historical books of the Jewish Bible–such as 1 and 2 Kings–describe with brutal honesty how ancient Israel did in fact dishonour their end of the bargain. They practised injustice and worshipped foreign deities. As a result, we are told, the Lord poured out the judgements he had threatened in Deuteronomy. This included not only the physical ailments but also banishment from the land of Israel. In 586 BC the Babylonians conquered Israel and exiled many inhabitants.

By the time of Jesus six centuries later, the Jews had returned to the Promised Land, but things had never fully recovered. They were ruled by the Persians during the sixth–fourth centuries BC, the Greeks from the fourth–second centuries and, although they enjoyed a brief period of self-determination in the second and first centuries BC, when the Romans came to power in Palestine in 63 BC that spelled the end of the Jewish state until 1948. In addition to these political hardships, Jews saw the evidence of the divine curses all around them: the blind, the lame, the lepers, the insane and the diseased. Signs of God's displeasure still lingered amongst his people.

But what has this précis of 1,500 years of biblical history got to do with John the Baptist's question about the "expected one" and Jesus' enigmatic reply outlining his baffling deeds? The answer is found in another set of promises in the Jewish Bible: this time not warnings about coming judgement, but pledges of glorious renewal. After the period of displeasure, says the prophet Isaiah, God will lift his curses and restore his people. He will bring the good news – the "gospel" – they have been waiting for:

> In that day the deaf will hear the words of the scroll,
>   and out of gloom and darkness
>   the eyes of the blind will see (Isaiah 29:18).

> Then will the eyes of the blind be opened
>   and the ears of the deaf unstopped.
> Then will the lame leap like a deer,
>   and the mute tongue shout for joy (Isaiah 35:5–6).

> The Spirit of the Sovereign LORD is on me,
>   because the LORD has anointed me to proclaim good
>   news to the poor.
> He has sent me to bind up the brokenhearted,
>   to proclaim freedom for the captives (Isaiah 61:1).

This is the context in which Jesus' reply to the Baptist can be seen to be brimming with Jewish significance. He answers his mentor's question, "Are you the one?" with a précis of his recent activity *deliberately couched in the language of Isaiah*: "Go back and report to John what you hear and see: The blind receive sight, the lame walk, those who have leprosy are cleansed, the deaf hear, the dead are raised, and the good news is proclaimed to the poor." Jesus' powers were not a party-trick designed to enhance his reputation; still less were they a model for the claims of contemporary faith-healers. They were a specific ministry to Israel, assuring the nation of God's favour and signalling the dawn of God's long-awaited kingdom.

A text from the famous Dead Sea Scrolls, written just before the time of Jesus, provides an extraordinary parallel to Jesus' words. It confirms that Jews in that period were looking forward to just the sort of things the man from Nazareth later claimed to do. The so-called *Messianic Apocalypse* was discovered at Qumran. Though fragmentary, the passage powerfully expresses the Jewish hope for a Messiah, an eternal kingdom and the healings and good news promised centuries earlier by the prophet Isaiah:

> ... the earth *will listen to his anointed one* (*mashiach* messiah) [and all] that is in them will not turn away from the precepts of the holy ones.... For he [the Lord] will honour the pious *upon the throne of an eternal kingdom*, freeing prisoners, giving *sight to the blind, straightening out the twis[ted.]* ... And the Lord will perform marvellous acts such as have not existed, just as he sa[id,] [for] he will *heal the badly wounded and will make the dead live*, he will *proclaim good news to the poor.*[16] (emphasis added)

This astonishing passage, which was not made readily available until the early 1990s, lays to rest any sceptical suggestion that Jesus' description of his work could only have been crafted after a period of sustained reflection on his life by later followers. No, this stuff was already in the air. As James Dunn rightly notes: "an expectation was current at the time of Jesus to the effect that the coming of God's Messiah would be accompanied by such marvellous events, in fulfilment of Isaiah's prophecies."[17]

But what was merely hoped for by the Essenes living down south in the desert region of the Dead Sea was, in Jesus' estimation, being realized up in Galilee as he healed and proclaimed good news to the poor. Evil was being expelled and lives were being restored; the future kingdom of God was being previewed before people's eyes.

As Jesus wandered Galilee teaching his band of disciples and offering healing to the crowds, I doubt any of them could have imagined what their story would become—a story embraced by over 2,000,000,000 people today. The tiny mustard seed Jesus planted somehow did inspire people to love amidst the violence and hatred of the world and to hope that God would one day make everything right. The mustard seed was becoming the kingdom.

CHAPTER 10

WHY DOESN'T GOD DO SOMETHING ABOUT THE MESS IN THE WORLD?

ALL THIS TALK ABOUT A KINGDOM IN WHICH GOD WILL RIGHT THE wrongs of the world, a kingdom in which love is the fundamental principle, raises obvious questions: Where is God in our pain? Why doesn't he do something about the mess in the world?

I do not claim expert status here. I myself ask this question regularly. In fact, though raised in a non-religious home, I first asked it when I was nine years old. A few days after my father was killed in a plane crash in India I approached my mother (so she tells me) with, "Why did God let Dad's plane crash?" I write this not to gain any sympathy or to establish any right to talk about pain, but simply to note how universal this question is. Even a child with no Christian input in his life, when faced with tragedy, knows the right question to ask: *why, God?*

This is not the book to explore all of the intricacies of this mind-bending and soul-troubling issue. I simply want to point out some of the things that have proved a comfort to me over the

Tank at Golan Heights in Palestine

years. I do not claim to have answers, but I think the Bible offers a few signposts pointing us in the right direction. I cling to the biblical understanding of suffering not because it has a knock-down argument about evil and pain, but because it seems to me the only viable option still standing.

QUESTIONING GOD

First, the Bible at least invites us to ask the question. Perhaps you don't feel you need permission to put your doubts and frustrations to the Almighty, but amongst the world religions Christianity (with its Jewish heritage) is unique in inviting sufferers to bring their complaints to God. Psalm 88 is raw in its pain and despair directed toward God:

> Why, LORD, do you reject me
>   and hide your face from me?
> From my youth I have suffered and been close to death;
>   I have borne your terrors and am in despair.
> Your wrath has swept over me;
>   your terrors have destroyed me (vv. 14 – 16).

Even more anguished are the opening lines of Psalm 22:

> My God, my God, why have you forsaken me?
>   Why are you so far from saving me,
>   so far from the words of my groaning?
> My God, I cry out by day, but you do not answer,
>   by night, but I find no rest (vv. 1 – 2).

If I followed the logic of Hinduism, such questioning would be inappropriate, for within the great Indian religious tradition all suffering is the result of "karma," the universal principle balancing actions with outcomes. Any particular example of suffering – whether the loss of a father or the descent into poverty – is the divinely sanctioned fruit of my own deeds. "As a man acts, as he behaves, so does he become," says one of the Upanishads, the main source of Hindu theology. "Whatever deeds he does on earth, their rewards he reaps. From the other world he comes back here – to the world of deed and work."[1]

If I followed the teaching of the Buddha, the question *why?* would prove I was far from enlightenment. Siddhartha Gautama insisted that all suffering arises because of desire. The desire for wealth makes poverty painful; the desire for pleasure makes hardship difficult; the desire for love makes the loss of a beloved father unbearable. Eradicate desire, said the Buddha, and all suffering ceases. This is the third of his Four Noble Truths – the Cessation of Suffering – "the complete cessation of that very desire, giving it up, relinquishing it, liberating oneself from it, and detaching oneself from it."[2]

Within Islam the cry of complaint to God is no less suspect. Indeed, it borders on blasphemy. At the heart of the world's second largest faith is a deep and abiding submission to the inscrutable will of Allah. "Islam" means "submission." For our Muslim friends all events are the direct activity of the finger of God. The Quran puts it succinctly: "Not a disaster befalls in the earth or in yourselves but is in a Book before we create it. That for Allah is an easy matter."[3] The reason an event is so determined in the Book of God is unknowable and unquestionable. Comfort is found in faithful resignation to the mystery of the divine will. Certainly, the cry "My God, my God, why have you forsaken me?" could not be part of the Islamic grammar of faith.

Nor is such language conceivable in an atheistic framework. One much-quoted statement of Richard Dawkins (which he has never sought to temper) puts it plainly:

> In a universe of blind physical forces and genetic replication, some people are going to get hurt, other people are going to get lucky, and we won't find any rhyme or reason in it, nor any justice. The universe we observe has precisely the properties we should expect if there is at the bottom no design, no purpose, no evil, and no good; nothing but blind, pitiless indifference. DNA neither knows, nor cares. DNA just is, and we dance to its music.[4]

Fortunately for the mental health of society, very few people really believe this rhetorical flourish, and those who do (such as Dawkins, I presume) probably get by in life precisely by *not* thinking of the universe in these terms. They might intellectually hold that there is no rhyme or reason, no purpose, evil or good, but they do not *act* as if that were true. In any case, my point here is that atheism rules out of court the question of suffering. Not only is there no ultimate purpose to be found in tragedy, there is no *One* out there to put the question to.

The Bible does not overrule the question of pain. Nor does it even discourage it. It invites us to come with anguished muscles full flexed and say "My God, why?" I suspect even faithful church-going folk might feel awkward echoing the sentiment of Psalm 22 (and many others like it). Many suppose that the only godly response to suffering is the one found in the very next psalm, the more famous Psalm 23: "The LORD is my shepherd, I lack nothing." But the presence of Psalm 22 in the Bible, immediately before Psalm 23, is a reminder that sometimes the cry "My God, why?" is just as spiritually valid as the affirmation "The LORD is my Shepherd."

THE GOD WHO HAS SUFFERED

If any further proof of this were needed, we only have to turn to the New Testament. There we find Jesus–the embodiment of God's reality–himself suffering injustice, agony and betrayal. And on the cross the words he chose to declare were not "The LORD is my shepherd" but the now-familiar opening lines of Psalm 22:

> And at three in the afternoon Jesus cried out in a loud voice, *"Eloi, Eloi, lema sabachthani?"* (which means "My God, my God, why have you forsaken me?") ... With a loud cry, Jesus breathed his last (Mark 15:34–37).

Here is the unique contribution of the New Testament to the biblical perspective on suffering. Not only are we humans invited to put the *why* question to the Almighty, God himself has entered into our world of injustice, sorrow and death. Jesus' cry from the cross was not an expression of self-doubt but a deliberate identification with anyone who has ever felt like screaming at the Creator. This does not resolve the problem of suffering; it doesn't even come close. But it does underline that the God to whom we bring our questions is involved not distant, tender not cold, himself wounded not dispassionate.

I felt the loss of my own father most when I was eighteen years old, long after he was gone. I began to see my own friends become friends with their fathers, and I was jealous. More than that, I was deeply resentful toward God for allowing my father to die.

"What do you know of my pain?" I asked in my head. "When have you ever known loss?" It turns out these questions have answers—in the shape of a cross. When I came to appreciate that, I did not suddenly find joy in suffering, but I did find immense comfort. I now understand that while I might not know God's reasons, I know his character. He is not the aloof puppeteer I had imagined; he is the deeply caring God who can identify with my anguish. He knows pain not just because he is all-knowing but because he has experienced it personally.

The Bible does promise a future kingdom when all injustice will be redressed, when all sickness will be removed and when death and evil will be overcome. That is the kingdom of God that Jesus preached and of which his miracles were a preview. But this is not simply a promise of pie-in-the-sky-when-you-die, as if Christianity were only about putting up with suffering now while we wait for the kingdom to come. God, in the Christian version, is present right now in our pain, and he calls on us to bring to him all of our doubts, frustrations and sorrow.

THREE QUESTIONS, TWO ANSWERS

There are really three questions we want to ask when faced with a tragedy. There is the question about the past: Why did it happen—what purpose could it serve? There is the question about the future: Will there be a resolution? And there is the question about the present: Where is the Almighty in our pain—in other words, does he care?

It seems to me that God, for reasons known only to him, has given answers to only *two* of these three questions. He has promised in the Bible that there will be a future resolution—a day when relationships will be restored and creation will be renewed. The book of Revelation promises, "There will be no more death or mourning or crying or pain, for the old order of things has passed away.... I am making everything new!"[5] That's the kingdom of God, and the resurrection of Jesus from the dead (discussed in chapter 17 of this book) is the ultimate sign and symbol of that renewal. But God has also given unmistakable evidence that he is with us now in our pain, that he is never closer than when we cry out to him *why?* The psalms of the Old Testament and the suffering of Jesus in the New Testament point us to a God who is tender and who himself bears wounds.

But so far as I can tell, the Bible has not revealed why any particular event in the past has occurred, apart from the general explanation that the tragedies of our world are a kind of reverberation of the rupture that has occurred between humanity and its Creator. We certainly are not encouraged to think of suffering as karmic payback, an illusion born of desire or the result of "blind, pitiless indifference," to use Dawkins' expression. None of these options is plausible to a reader of the Bible.

Are we not told why painful events happen because the reasons are so many and varied for them to be listed in Scripture, or because the reason is beyond our imagining? I do not know. But one thing I do know is that God has answered the two more important questions about our pain. Ponder this. If we were allowed to know the answers to just *two* of the three questions of suffering – *Why* did it happen? Will it be *resolved*? Does God *care*? – wouldn't we all choose the latter two? Wouldn't we prefer to know whether God intends to resolve our pain (the question about the future) and whether he cares for us in our pain (the question about the present)?

Imagine my knowing why my father died and how it would be resolved but not knowing whether God is with me in my pain right now. On the other hand, imagine knowing why it happened and that God cares but not knowing whether there will be an end to pain, a resolution to suffering. Knowing why might satisfy our curiosity and intellect, and help clergymen sound more learned at funerals, but not knowing whether there will be a resolution to suffering would leave us without real hope, and not knowing whether the Creator grieves with us in our pain would leave us without his immediate comfort. As it is, Jesus' teaching about the renewal of all things in the kingdom of God fosters hope as we endure pain, and his anguished crucifixion reminds us not only that we are free to confront God with our pain but also that the One to whom we bring our doubts, frustrations and sorrow is compassionate, sympathetic and himself acquainted with grief. For me that makes all the difference.

JUDGE AND FRIEND

Jesus' Thoughts on "Religious Hypocrites"
and "Rotten Sinners"

CHAPTER 11

HELL-FIRE AND BRIMSTONE

THERE IS A TEMPTATION IN POPULAR DISCUSSION – AND SOMETIMES in academia – to make Jesus a softly spoken social activist who only preached love and acceptance. In reality, Jesus said some things that would give the fire-and-brimstone fundamentalist a run for his money. This is not to say fundamentalist Christianity reflects the Jesus of history better than the liberal version does – both are capable of fashioning Jesus into their own image. But on the topic of divine punishment the traditionalists have preserved something the historian unfortunately cannot avoid. Jesus preached judgement.

Many of us are familiar with the "good news" Jesus announced throughout Galilee – "blessed are the meek" and "blessed are the peacemakers." But there was a flip side that is not so popular. At the core of Jesus' vision – straight out of the Old Testament – was the promise that the kingdom of God was coming. That kingdom, as I have said several times, would establish justice and love and, in so doing, would sweep away everything that was contrary to

Chorazin, a
town in Galilee
denounced
by Jesus

God's purposes. The good news of the kingdom was also bad news for those who opposed it.

The evidence that Jesus, like John the Baptist before him, warned of God's impending judgement is overwhelming. More than thirty passages from the earliest Gospel sources record Jesus speaking on judgement. As clichéd as it may sound, Jesus said God was coming to judge the wicked. Against those on the fringe of scholarship who try to rearrange the sources to produce a "non-judging" Jesus, Dale Allison, a leading Jesus scholar, remarks:

> [The earliest sources of the Gospels] would seem to speak for themselves, and to speak volumes. This material reflects the conviction that God's judgement is coming, and that it is coming soon. Is all of it incongruent with Jesus' proclamation? Surely here is a theme that is so much a part of the tradition that, were one to deny it to Jesus, the very possibility of the modern quest would fall into disrepute for the reason that the sources are too untrustworthy.[1]

In other words, Jesus-preaching-judgement is so widely attested in our earliest sources that, if one wants to reject this element of the narrative, one might as well reject the whole thing.

So, to whom did Jesus direct his warnings? At the top of his list of Destined-for-Judgement were the self-righteous and the hypocrites. Jesus once said:

> Woe to you Pharisees, because you give a tenth of your mint and rue and all your herbs, but you overlook justice and the love of God. Woe to you Pharisees, because you love the best seat in the synagogues, and the way people greet you in the market place. Woe to you religious lawyers as well! For you load people up with burdens that are hard to carry, but you yourselves will not lift one finger to bear the load (Luke 11:42–46).

The word "woe" sounds quaint today, but in the original Aramaic it meant "disaster." God was about to ruin the hypocritical religious leaders. The "meek and mild" Jesus of popular imagination does not really square with the portrait left in our earliest sources.

But Jesus did not direct his warnings only at the religious professionals. He believed the rank and file of the towns and villages around him were also in grave danger of falling under the judgement of God. Speaking of cities that had witnessed Jesus' miracles but were rejecting his call for love, Jesus again spoke of great "woe":

> I say to you that it will be more tolerable for Sodom
> on the day of judgement than for that city. Woe to you,
> Chorazin; woe to you, Bethsaida! For if the powerful deeds
> that have happened in you had taken place in Tyre and
> Sidon long ago, they would have repented in sackcloth and
> ashes. But it will be more tolerable for Tyre and Sidon in the
> judgement than for you. And you, Capernaum, will you be
> lifted up to the heavens? No, you will go down to hell (Luke
> 10:12–15).

I have stood in the ruins of both Chorazin and Capernaum. I tried to imagine what it was like to hear Jesus say this sort of thing. Some must have thought him mad: "How could God intend to treat us worse than the horrible pagans living in Tyre or Sidon!" I suspect others, convinced of Jesus' absolute integrity and nearness to God, began to search their hearts and fear the worst.

THE REASONS FOR JUDGEMENT

What was Jesus so concerned about? How had people so failed God's standards that they were now to be punished? The answer, often the case in Jesus' teaching, has to do with love. In Jesus' view people had replaced God's commands with their own cultural norms and traditions. They were pandering to the rich, trampling on the poor and pursuing a path of intolerance and violence. In short, they had not loved God or their neighbour – and, for Jesus, that is what life here on earth was all about.

He was once asked a favourite theological question of the time: "Which is the greatest of God's commandments?" The Pharisees had counted 613 commandments in Scripture, so there were quite a few to choose from. Jesus quoted just two: "Love God with all your heart" and "love your neighbour as yourself"

(Mark 12:28–31). This teaching was once quoted back at him by a religious scholar.

> A certain expert in the Jewish law stood up, wanting to test Jesus. "Teacher," he said, "What must I do so that I will inherit eternal life?" And Jesus said to him, "What is written in the Law? How do you read it?" The lawyer replied, "Love the Lord your God with all your heart and with all your soul and with all your strength and with all your mind; and love your neighbour as yourself." Jesus said to him, "You have answered correctly. Do this, and you will live" (Luke 10:25–28).

According to Jesus, the Golden Rule of God's kingdom is a simple, two-fold directive: love your Maker and love your neighbour. Jesus was not the first to speak in this way. There is a near parallel to Jesus' teaching in a Jewish text called the *Testament of Issachar* written in Syria (or perhaps Egypt) a century and a half earlier:

> Keep the Law of God, my children; achieve integrity; live without malice, not tinkering with God's commands or your neighbor's affairs. Love the Lord and your neighbor; be compassionate toward poverty and sickness. Bend your back in farming, perform the tasks of the soil in every kind of agriculture, offering gifts to the Lord.[2]

The parallel is not exact. The exhortation to love God and neighbour appears in the middle of a host of other instructions, including to "achieve integrity" and to "bend your back in farming," rather than as the central command. We do not know if Jesus was the first to express the double commandment as the greatest commandment. All we know is that this Jewish stress on the importance of love came to intense expression in Jesus' teaching.

In any case, the logic of this double command to love God and neighbour is seamless. If God exists, what could be more central to life than loving devotion to our Creator and compassion toward our fellow creatures? What I find so striking about the teaching is the way it leaves no room either for the religious hypocrite or for the moral agnostic. The religious hypocrite loves God but cares little for others. The moral agnostic is decent toward neighbours but ignores God, the source of life itself. We rightly condemn the hypocrite, but on Jesus' teaching the moral agnostic is no less culpable. Both fail God's demands.

Many in contemporary society think of sin as the petty vices *others* get up to. There is a convenience to this understanding. It allows those of us who do not commit many of these vices to think of ourselves as basically good people, and those who do enjoy the odd vice or two think God petty for worrying about such trivial things. Jesus' understanding, however, was less convenient. Petty vices are hardly what make one a sinner, and the avoidance of vices does not make one good. God's standard was love – for him and our fellow creatures.

I once had a very interesting dinner party discussion with a lawyer. He asked what I did for a living, which tends either to kill or energize the conversation. I explained, and he promptly responded with, "Oh, I don't feel I need religion. I'm a decent person." Overlooking the implication that, since I had religion, I must not be a decent person, I asked "By whose definition?" "What do you mean?" he replied. "You said you were a decent person," I said. "I'm just wondering on what definition." He was a lawyer, so you could almost hear his brain clicking through the logical options. "By my own definition," he said firmly. Appropriate to the cheeky tone of the conversation I said, "Well, that's easy, isn't it? You invent the definition and uncannily find yourself within it!" He went on to explain how he tried to treat others how he'd like to be treated. He as good as quoted Jesus without knowing it. "Well, what's your definition?" he asked. I said that I preferred to borrow one from Jesus and explained that he had insisted treating others well was only half of the definition. We were to love neighbour *and* God. I pointed out that, while we were at liberty to invent our own definitions of good and bad, my money was on Jesus getting such things right. We agreed to disagree, but I am pretty sure I detected a little unease in his voice as he found himself claiming in essence that his definition of goodness was superior to that of Jesus of Nazareth.

My point is that loving neighbour is not the whole of the ethical life. Jesus insisted it must also include loving our Creator. We are right to censure the religious hypocrite who loves God but does not care for people. But, as I said, I'm not sure Jesus would see the reverse as any less problematic. To treat other creatures well but neglect the Creator of life itself cannot, on Jesus' teaching, be more acceptable than religious hypocrisy.

The modern fundamentalist may have abused the themes of sin and judgement and turned them into awful clichés. But there is no question, the Jesus of history declared judgement on all who refused to love God and neighbour.

CHAPTER 12

FRIEND OF SINNERS

JESUS' EMPHASIS ON HUMAN SIN AND DIVINE PUNISHMENT HAS TO be balanced with another, seemingly contradictory, aspect of his life. He befriended those we might have thought were first in line for the "fires" of judgement. He was even slandered in public over this issue, with some openly declaring, "Look, he's a glutton and a drunkard, a friend of tax collectors and sinners" (Luke 7:34).

All scholars agree: one of Jesus' most striking habits was to associate with the immoral and irreligious–those classed "sinners." The word "sinner" sounds clichéd now, but in the first century it was a potent insult. The *Psalms of Solomon*, a Jewish text written by Pharisees in Jerusalem shortly before the time of Jesus, conveys well the contemporary attitudes toward sinners:

> The sinner stumbles and curses his life, the day of his birth, and his mother's pains. He adds sin upon sin in his life; he falls–his fall is serious–and he will not get up. The destruction of the sinner is forever, and he will not be remembered

First-century
house at
Nazareth Village

when God looks after the righteous. This is the share of the sinners forever.[1]

The document goes on to describe how the hoped-for Messiah, the Lord's righteous King, would utterly condemn and destroy the world's sinful rebels. I think we can say with some confidence that Jesus' habit of associating with sinners and tax collectors, even making "friends" with them, was not exactly Messiah-like. It was yet another way in which Jesus refused to fit with first-century expectations of his role as the Anointed One.

WHO WERE THE "TAX COLLECTORS"?

A particular kind of sinner frequently mentioned in the story of Jesus is the tax collector. In the public slander just quoted Jesus is described as "friend of tax collectors." Elsewhere, the Pharisees ask "Why does he eat with tax collectors and sinners?"[2] Who were these officials?

There were two broad types of taxes in this period: those paid directly to the state of Rome (usually called tribute) and a multitude of indirect duties on imports and exports. Needless to say, the system was not as carefully monitored as modern taxes are and was open to abuse by those in charge. The first-century Jewish writer Philo describes the rapid success of a tribute collector named Capito, who was active shortly after Jesus:

> Capito is the tax-collector for Judaea and cherishes a spite against the population. When he came there he was a poor man but by his rapacity and peculation he has amassed much wealth in various forms.[3]

The tax collectors we meet in the Gospels were probably not tribute collectors like Capito but simple customs officers who gathered the various indirect taxes.[4] Nevertheless, in a district like Galilee, which produced a lot of Palestine's foodstuff, the person in charge of the levies on imports and exports could, if he chose, make a very pretty profit at the expense of others. As Prof Joachim Jeremias of the University of Leipzig noted, they "exploited public ignorance of the scale of tolls to administer duties unscrupulously into their own pockets during their tax season."[5] It is in this context that tax collectors gained a reputation for greed and corruption. The Roman aristocrat and chronicler Suetonius around AD 120 describes how Emperor Vespasian's father, Sabinus, had collected the import/export taxes in Asia Minor (present-day Turkey). He reports how numerous statues had been erected in his honour throughout the region bearing the inscription *kalōs telōnēsanti*, "to an honest tax collector" (Suetonius, *Life of Vespasian* 1.2–3). The inscription indicates that some tax collectors were considered trustworthy, and that this was worthy of special note!

Bleeding the poor on behalf of the rich contravened a core principle of Jewish ethics,[6] and so it is no wonder that tax collectors came to be associated with the general class of "sinners." That some of the indirect levies probably contributed to Rome's coffers may also have made it easy to think of tax collectors as collaborators with the pagan occupiers.

It is striking, then, that sometimes Jesus *takes the initiative* in urging tax collectors to be his disciples:

> Jesus entered Jericho and was passing through it. There was a man there named Zacchaeus, a senior tax collector, who was rich. He was trying to see who Jesus was, but he was unable to, because he was a small man and the crowd got in the way. He ran ahead of the crowd, and climbed up a fig tree to see him, because Jesus was about to pass by that way. When Jesus got to that place, he looked up and said to him, "Zacchaeus, climb down now, because I have to stay in your home today." He climbed down quickly and welcomed Jesus gladly into his home. When everyone saw this, they complained, "He has gone to stay with a man who is a sinner" (Luke 19:1–7).

Here, again, we find the controversial issue of socializing or dining with sinners. Why was this such a problem?

THE MEANING OF MEALS

One very clear difference between contemporary society and ancient Mediterranean life was the relative significance of the meal. Today, eating and drinking can take place just about anywhere and with just about anyone. We do enjoy our culinary adventures, but this mostly has to do with epicurean delight—the taste of the food, the ambience of the venue, the laughter of friends and so on – rather than with the social-spiritual significance of dining. But in Jesus' day eating with someone was far more than a convenient way to fill your stomach: it was a real social statement. You normally only sat down at a table with those you wanted to honour as family and equals. As a result, there were quite strict rules against eating with the immoral or irreligious. Writing in Jerusalem in 132 BC, Jesus son of Sira (Ben Sira) taught, "Let the righteous be your dinner companions"[7] and "Do not invite everyone into your home, for many are the tricks of the crafty."[8] More tellingly, he noted:

> All living beings associate with their own kind, and people stick close to those like themselves. What does a wolf have in common with a lamb? No more has a sinner with the devout.[9]

The Essenes of Qumran offer a more extreme example.[10] Before eating the regular community meal known as the "Pure Food," members of the sect were required to change into linen clothing and wash in a ritual bath (*mikveh*). After the meal, they changed back into their tunic and carried on the day's work. Novices were not allowed to join this common table for twelve months. Even full members could be excluded, and have their rations withheld if they were found to have sinned. We read in the *Rule of the Community*: "If one is found among them who has lied knowingly concerning possessions, he shall be excluded from the pure food of the Many [i.e., the community] for a year and they shall withhold a quarter of his bread."[11] Josephus reports that banished members sometimes even starved to death because an Essene "is not at liberty to partake of other men's food."[12] Jesus had a very different view:

> Levi held a great feast for Jesus at his house, with a large crowd of tax collectors; and others were there as well, reclining at the table with them. Now the Pharisees and Scribes complained to Jesus' disciples, "Why do you eat and drink with tax collectors and sinners?" And Jesus replied, "It is not the healthy who need a doctor, but the sick. I have not come to invite the righteous, but sinners to repentance" (Luke 5:29–32).

Jesus was not approving of the behaviour of sinners, as the religious leaders feared. He was trying to send a powerful message about the kingdom of God. Yes, the kingdom would overthrow all who rejected the path of love, but until then God offered amnesty to all who wanted it. Jesus' controversial meals were a symbol of the forgiveness he believed God held out to sinners before the day of judgement.

CHAPTER 13

JESUS ON SIN, GOD AND RELIGION

THE PARABLE OF THE PRODIGAL SON IS ONE OF JESUS' MOST FAMOUS stories. Luke introduces the passage by telling us that Jesus told the parable as a reply to the grumbling of the religious leaders: "The Pharisees and the Scribes were grumbling and saying, 'This man welcomes sinners and eats meals with them.' So he told them this parable" (Luke 15:2–3). Then follows this extraordinary hypothetical. It is worth quoting at length because here Jesus tells us so much about what he thinks of sin, religion and God:

> There was a man who had two sons. The younger one said to his father, "Father, give me my share of the inheritance." The father then divided the property between the two sons. Soon afterwards, the younger son collected everything together and travelled to a distant land, where he squandered his inheritance on reckless living. After he had spent everything, there was a great famine in that land, and he began to be in need. So he went and hired himself out to a

Jerusalem

citizen of that land, who sent him out to his fields to feed pigs. And he was longing to feed himself with the pods that the pigs were eating; yet no-one gave him anything. Then he came to his senses and thought, "How many of my father's employees have an abundance of food, and yet here am I dying of hunger. I'll get up and go to my father and say to him, 'I have sinned toward God and before you. I am no longer worthy to be called your son. Make me like one of your employees.'" So he got up and went to his father.

He was still some distance away when his father caught sight of him. The father was deeply moved, and running to his son he embraced him and kissed him. The son said, "Father, I have sinned toward God and before you. I am no longer worthy to be called your son."

But the father said to his servants, "Quick, bring out the best robe and dress him in it; put a ring on his finger and shoes on his feet. Bring the fattened calf and kill it. Let's eat and celebrate, because this son of mine was dead but now is alive again; he was lost but now is found." And they began to celebrate.

Now the elder son had been in the field, and as he drew near the house he heard music and dancing. And calling one of the hired hands, he asked what this was all about. He replied, "Your brother has come and your father has killed the fattened calf, because he has got him back safe and well." The elder son became furious and refused even to enter the house. But his father went outside and pleaded with him. He answered his father, "Look! I have been slaving for you for so many years, and I have never disobeyed your command. Yet you have never given me even a goat so that I could have a celebration with my friends. But when this son of yours, who has squandered your estate on prostitutes, comes home, you kill the fattened calf for him!" But his father said to him, "My child, you are always with me, and everything that is mine is yours. But we must celebrate and rejoice, because this brother of yours was dead but now is alive, and was lost but now is found" (Luke 15:11–31).

Just as there are three characters in this parable, so Jesus was trying to make three points. The younger son obviously represents the "sinners" in Jesus' audience. The elder brother represents the complaining religious folk of the day. The father is of course God. In these few paragraphs Jesus gives us his own perspective on sinners, religion and the nature of the Almighty.

The description of the young son is telling. While we often think of sin in terms of vices, as I said in the previous chapter, Jesus casts it in terms of relationship. The real offence offered by the son to his father was not the later "reckless living" but the way he wanted everything his father had to offer—the family inheritance—and nothing to do with the father himself. He took the father's wealth and spent it on himself in a foreign land. This is a compelling picture of the sinner, the one who wants everything God has to offer—food, wealth, relationships, sex, technology, and all the other gifts of our Maker—but nothing to do with God himself. In my family, having a "good" son who did his homework, did jobs around the house and who was not mixed up in a bad crowd would mean very little if he never talked to me—*that* is what would break my heart more than any particular vice. In the West we are world experts at enjoying the good things of creation while ignoring the Creator. We neglect to thank God for these things, fail to seek his wishes for how they should be used and refuse to apologise for their misuse. In short, we do not love God. (And when we hoard the gifts of creation for ourselves, we are not loving our neighbours either.) We are sinners, living at a distance.

But Jesus not only has an intriguing picture of the sinner here in this parable; he also has a compelling portrait of God. For many in his audience, the turning point in the story, where the sinful son decides to return to the father, would have provoked expectations of fatherly punishment. But this father runs, embraces and kisses the returning son before the son has even blurted out the apology. And when the repentant young man does offer his confession, the father interrupts him mid-sentence to call for the robe, the ring and the fattened calf. These are signs of lavish acceptance, not parental discipline. This is Jesus' picture of God and it provides a stunning contrast to the grumbling religion—depicted by the "furious" elder brother—of his day. It also offers a deliberate explanation of his scandalous meals and friendships with the sinners of his day. According to Jesus, at the first sign of a sinner's return God will accept and forgive. And contrary to the opinion of many, God is not in the business of stifling our lives and limiting our enjoyment of his goodness. He wishes to lavish his mercy and kindness on us. God–so says Jesus–is a running, embracing, forgiving, celebrating parent. Jesus' meals with the immoral were signs of the welcoming grace of the Creator.

LOSING MY RELIGION

Obviously, the elder brother in this story represents the Pharisees and scribes who, Luke told us at the start, were grumbling over Jesus' welcoming attitude toward "sinners." As such, Jesus' description provides fascinating insight into how Jesus pictured religion.

First, this elder brother is a kill-joy. As the text says, he "became furious and refused even to enter the house" and join the party. Throughout the Gospels there is a deliberate contrast between the parties and joy associated with Jesus and the morbid grumbling of the religious leaders. The public complaint about Jesus quoted in the previous chapter says it all: "he's a glutton and a drunkard, a friend of tax collectors and sinners" (Luke 7:34). So when we get to the parable of the prodigal son, it is clear that Jesus is deliberately contrasting the joy associated with his vision of faith (a party thrown by the father) and the morbid outlook of religion (the grumbling of the elder son). Religion, in other words, refuses to join the celebration that is faith in Jesus Christ.

When your religion is fundamentally about rules there will be very little joy in life. This is partly because you never really know if you've done enough to please God and partly because to the extent you think you might have done enough, you will be annoyed at all those who have not. Unfortunately, this seems to be the only sort of Christian that New Atheists like Christopher Hitchens and Michel Onfray have ever met. The impression they give in their writings is that Christianity is fundamentally morbid, life-denying, joy-killing. Prof Onfray in his *Atheist Manifesto* writes:

> The religion of the one God espouses these impulses. It seeks to promote self-hatred to the detriment of the body, to discredit the intelligence, to despise the flesh, and to prize everything that stands in the way of a gratified subjectivity. Launched against others, it foments contempt.[1]

I don't doubt that there are such Christians, but this is the opposite of what Jesus taught. For Jesus, God's love (not rules) is at the centre. As a result, the basic experience of true faith is joy. Not mere happiness; it is entirely possible to be in the midst of sorrow and depression and still be joyful. Christian joy is a confident assurance in the knowledge that at the centre of everything is not a load of rules but a God of love.

This leads to Jesus' second criticism of religion in this parable. Religion turns you into a slave. The son's response to his father says it all: "Look! I have been slaving for you for so many years, and I have never disobeyed your command" (Luke 15:29). By his own confession, this young man adopts the stance of a slave to a master, not a son to a father. Here we confront one of Jesus' most stinging criticisms of first-century religious life. He thought the religious were enslaved by the sheer number of their regulations. On one occasion he said "Woe to you religious lawyers as well! For you load people up with burdens that are hard to carry, but you yourselves will not lift one finger to bear the load" (Luke 11:46). Jesus was talking about the myriad laws developed in Judaism of this period, laws that were eventually compiled in the Mishnah, the second great holy book of Orthodox Judaism today. Consider the following mishnaic laws about ritual hand washing (a theme over which Jesus also clashed with the Pharisees[2]):

> The hands are susceptible to uncleanness and are rendered clean up to the wrist. How so? If one poured the first water [of two compulsory cleansings] up to the wrist, and the second beyond the wrist and it went back to the hand – it is clean. If he poured out the first and the second pouring of water beyond the wrist and it went back to the hand, it is unclean. If he poured out the first water onto one hand, and was reminded and poured out the second water on to both hands, they are unclean. If he poured out the first water on to both hands and was reminded and poured out the second water on to one hand, his hand, which has been washed twice, it is clean. If he poured out water on to one hand and rubbed it on the other, it is unclean (Mishnah *Yadayim* 2.3).

I want to say something that is a little controversial but I think irrefutable. Christianity is by far the least regulated of all world religions. Orthodox Judaism has the commands not only of the Old Testament, but also of the Mishnah and another law book called the Talmud. Islam has both the rulings of the Quran and the vast body of regulations found in the Hadiths – laws about the correct way to pray, eat, conduct war and so on. The fixed legal code of Islam (Shariah) would fill several bookshelves. Hinduism has the *dharma sutras*, an extensive collection of writings describing the moral and ritual duties of each caste in Hindu society. And perhaps no other religion is as mentally and ethically demanding as Buddhism. How wrong was the young man I once overheard at a dinner party who criticized what he called "the burdens of Western religion," by which he meant Christianity, and praised Buddhism because "it offers me spirituality without any obligations." He said this as he sipped his chardonnay, unaware that the Buddha forbade alcohol, unaware too that the goal of Buddhism is the complete cessation of human desire.

None of this is intended to criticize these faiths. I value the world religions enough to have taught them for several years at university level. In any case, adherents of these faiths would basically agree with what I am saying. And they would defend their level of ritual and ethical regulation by saying that it is a privilege, not a burden, to have every aspect of life – from eating to praying, from fighting to resting – regulated by sacred authority. All I am saying here is that Christianity, following Jesus, sees things differently. For Jesus, a life dominated by rules turns a child into a slave: "I have been slaving for you for so many years," said the elder brother in Jesus' parable.

Of course, this is not to say that Jesus did not have any expectations. He was not some ultra-liberal life coach who just wanted us to accept ourselves and each other as we are and be happy. Five minutes in the Gospels makes that clear. In fact, this parable of the prodigal son makes that clear. In no sense is the younger son in the parable (Jesus' picture of the sinner) fine just as he was. He had demanded his father's wealth, kept his distance from the father and then squandered the family inheritance on himself. Here, then, is the interesting thing. It is true that over-regulating your spiritual life is enslaving, but completely de-regulating your life is not any better. The older son might have been enslaved by his fixation on rules. But the younger son is not exactly free in his rejection of them. There he was, according to Jesus' narrative, hiring himself out to a pig farmer (which in ancient Jewish society was about as desperate as you can get).

TRUE FREEDOM

Living free of any spiritual or moral claim on your life is just another kind of slavery. Think of money. Buying everything you want is not freedom; it is captivity to what Alain de Botton calls "status anxiety," and you know you've got it when yesterday's luxuries seem like today's necessities.[3] Or take the sexual realm. Having sex with whomever you wish is not freedom; it is a kind of subservience to one of your least reliable and clear-headed desires. Or in relationships generally: treating others however you want is not freedom; it is a recipe for damaging the best things in your life. Freedom is not doing whatever you want. It is the capacity to be what you are made for. As David Bentley Hart puts it in his *Atheist Delusions*:

> True human freedom is emancipation from whatever con-
> strains us from living the life of rational virtue, or from expe-
> riencing the full fruition of our nature; and among the things
> that constrain us are our own untutored passions; our willful
> surrender to momentary impulses, our own foolish or wicked
> choices. In this view of things, we are free when we achieve
> that end toward which our inmost nature is oriented, and
> whatever separates us from that end—even if it comes from
> our own wills—is a form of bondage. We become free, that is,
> in something of the same way that (in Michelangelo's image)
> the form is "liberated" from the marble by the sculptor. This
> means we are free not merely because we can choose, but only
> when we have chosen well. For to choose poorly, through
> folly or malice, in a way that thwarts our nature and distorts
> our proper form, is to enslave ourselves to the transitory, the
> irrational, the purposeless, the (to be precise) subhuman.[4]

To put it in less rarified terms, a fish is only free in water—the "freedom" to be out of the water is only freedom in the most absurd sense. A bird is only free when it follows the laws of aero-dynamics. Otherwise, it is freefalling, which is not the same thing as being free. Or think of the rules of surfing, a sport I have picked up again after a twenty-five-year hiatus. There are a few things I remember from my teenage surfing exploits: get up quick, ride across the wave not straight down it, and place your weight at the back. Deciding to get up slowly, go straight down the wave and stand at the front of the board is not an expression of freedom – it is called getting dunked. The rules of art and music illustrate the same thing. It is attention to certain rules that creates the thing of beauty. Any singer will tell you that you are most free when you are most in tune and in the groove with the band.

It goes without saying that over-regulating your surfing or art or music is soul-destroying and joy-sapping. But avoiding the rules altogether is a mess. It is the same with faith, according to Jesus. To fixate on rules is to become a slave within the household. To reject all rules is to become a hired hand in a distant land. But God wants children. I find it so interesting that the father in this famous parable is tender to both sons.

His tenderness to the younger son (the picture of the "sinners") is legendary. His tenderness to the older son (the picture of the "religious") is no less real. When the son refuses to join the party, the father does not rebuke him; he pleads with him to join in. And when the son bites back with, "You have never given me even a goat so that I could have a celebration with my friends," the father is patient, pointing out the reality that everything – the goat, the robe, the fattened calf, etc. – was all there for his enjoyment: "My child, you are always with me, and everything that is mine is yours." Religion does that: when you are obsessed with rules, you never know if you have done enough to enjoy the Almighty's favour. Religion blinds you to God's goodness and keeps you from relaxing in his love. It keeps you a slave. God does not want us to put rules at the centre. Nor does he want us putting ourselves at the centre. He wants us to place his love at the centre – and to let that be the regulator of life. That, after all, is what we are made for, and in that is true freedom.

GETTING THE BALANCE RIGHT

We are left with a paradox in the life of Jesus. The man who regularly proclaimed God's judgement befriended those under judgement. Throughout history people have tried to resolve this tension by focusing on only one part of Jesus' teaching. Some think only of his inclusiveness; others prefer his warnings. However, we must try to hold both threads together. Jesus preached both divine judgement and divine mercy. He thundered out his warnings about the coming woe but sat down at the table to offer his mercy.

The first Christians, of course, had no problem holding these thoughts together. For them, the paradox was resolved not in Jesus' life but in his death. On the cross, they said, Jesus bore the judgement sinners deserve. What his meals with sinners symbolised, his death would secure.

There is an important balance to get right here. One of the inescapable teachings of the Christian faith is that God will require people to give an account of their lives—that God will judge us. For some, this conjures up an image of an old man in a wig sitting on high while we cower in front of him, watching him read the diaries of our deeds, words and thoughts (or, worse still, viewing the DVD!). It is hardly something we look forward to.

But on reflection, I would hazard to say that we all want judgement to take place—at least for other people if not for ourselves! We want to see justice done. We want to see murderers and tyrants punished but, equally, we hope we ourselves are treated mercifully. We might also feel that a concept of judgement has a helpful restraining effect on human behaviour. It is a good thing that people have an awareness of being judged—whether by earthly or divine forces—for, otherwise, we are inclined to treat each other even more poorly.

It might be a horrifying thought to think of God judging the world, but it is more horrifying to think that there will be no judgement—no calling people to account for abusing children in secret, for stealing money from pensioners, for starting wars or for bashing wives. Surely, most of us want to see justice, even if we find it hard to imagine what capital-J Judgement might look like.

The Christian idea of sin makes a lot of sense of the world. Sin is that attitude and state of our hearts that produces evil words, evil deeds, evil thoughts. It's the prison we find ourselves in, even when we want to be better. The theologian Alistair McFadyen in his Cambridge University Press publication *Bound to Sin* argued that the Bible's concept of sin does a better job of explaining why the Holocaust took place, or why a father sexually abuses his stepdaughter than does any social or psychological theory.[5] It explains why hurtful, harmful behaviour has an addictive character to it, and why we are able to convince ourselves (under the right conditions) that the most atrocious acts of inhumanity are in fact acceptable. It is a deep-down-inside wrongness in the human condition that brings about these atrocities. And so – at least in theory – we want there to be a reckoning, a judgement.

On the other hand, we want to avoid all talk of judgement, because we suspect it might come down hard on us, too. That's where the message of Christianity comes in – God shows us mercy when he ought to judge us. Because of Jesus' death on our behalf, discussed in the next chapter, God's requirement of justice is satisfied and we can be shown mercy. It is the biggest relief and the most stunning achievement of twin-goods: the price of justice is paid and the victims are avenged, while the unjust can also be forgiven and set free.

There is no doubt that the church has often failed people in this area. Too often we hear priests and bishops and everyday Christians telling people almost gleefully that they are going to hell. These themes have been used to place people in a state of guilt as a means of control. That is a perversion of the teaching of Jesus, to be sure. But that doesn't mean there isn't a version of the theme that is true to Jesus' message. Yes, he taught about sin and hell. But this message of judgement should be given in tears, just like Jesus shed tears over Jerusalem as he announced that it, too, would be judged:

> As Jesus came near and saw the city, he wept over it. He said, "How I wish that you – you of all places – had recognised this day the things that bring peace! But now they are hidden from your eyes. For days are coming upon you when your enemies will set up a barricade against your walls. They will surround you and trap you from every side. They will destroy you and your children within your walls, and they will not leave one single stone upon another within you. And all this because you did not recognise the time of your visitation" (Luke 19:41 – 44).

There are the tears of grief for those who fall under God's judgement, tears of guilt in acknowledging personal failure, and then there are the tears of joy for those who find forgiveness and mercy by confessing their sin to God and being saved from the judgement that is coming.

It is sometimes said that one of the major reasons we recoil at the thought of judgement is very basic psychology: we don't like being in trouble. In fact, we so dislike the feeling of disapproval and reprimand, that we will modify our beliefs in order to alleviate ourselves of what scientists of the mind call "cognitive dissonance." People often throw this at Christians in the form of: "You just can't cope with life (that's the dissonance), so you invent a Father-in-the-Sky to make things better." But this cuts both ways. One could just as easily say: "You don't like the idea of a God of justice watching the world (dissonance), so you invent a version of the deity that only ever approves of your actions." The real issue is not so much which thought relieves which dissonance, but which idea is *true*.

Some prefer the deist image of God. Deism, as discussed in chapter 1, teaches that God began the universe, but has had no role in it since. On this view, God is more like a principle than a person, or more like an author than an actor: he wrote the Book, but has nothing to do with it after that. This means that God wouldn't really care about our lives, and certainly wouldn't stand in judgement of them. God has no more interest in people's lives than does a watchmaker in the ticking of the clocks he has wound up and sold.

The distant God of deism may make us feel the sense of relief you get when you get away with telling a lie, but that is nothing compared to the relief of admitting our failings and finding that we are loved by the Almighty all the same. The distant God is surely second best to one who does indeed care, who promises to judge, but who also promises to forgive the wrongs of those who turn to him.

Christians have certainly made mistakes when they have spoken about judgement. They have often emphasised the horrors of being judged, rather than the love of God in showing mercy to sinners. Some preachers so stress the Bible's teaching on hell (often distorting it in the process) that they give the impression that God wants to condemn people. In fact, the Bible teaches the opposite: God desires not the death of a sinner, rather that he should turn from his wickedness and live (Ezekiel 18:32). Any talk of judgement then ought to be done through tears and out of love for those who are listening, because that is the Christian way. It is certainly what Jesus taught and embodied.

WHAT ABOUT THOSE WHO HAVE NEVER HEARD?

All of this raises a question many of us have pondered over the years: What about those who have never heard – will they be condemned just because they weren't fortunate enough to hear about God's offer of salvation in Jesus? Let me be frank and say that the Bible does not give all of the information I might have liked on this issue. Some things are clear, others vague.

First, I should make clear that I do not believe anyone will be condemned by God *for not having heard about Jesus*. That would be absurd and a serious challenge to the Bible's teaching that God is fair. How could he punish the woman in central Afghanistan for failing to accept a message she has never heard and has very little chance of ever hearing? It is unthinkable. That said, nor do I believe that "sincerity of belief" is the criterion of God's acceptance. You often hear this said (sometimes by Christians even): "So long as people are sincere in their beliefs, God will be merciful to them." I cannot agree. Sincerity is a very slippery concept. Where do you draw the line? Will God accept the "sincere" suicide bomber who wants to enter Paradise by taking out as many infidels as he or she can? What about the ancient Canaanite who sincerely believed that children should be sacrificed in the fire to the deity Molech? Can the Creator look favourably on that because the sacrifice was sincere? I truly hope not. Sincerity cannot be the criterion of God's treatment of those who have not heard.

So, what is the criterion of God's judgement of those who don't know about Christianity? God will judge people by an utterly fair principle: how they responded to the truth that they knew. The Afghani woman, to continue the example, will not be scrutinized over her response to an unknown message but over *what she did* with *what she knew*. Which of course raises the question: What does she know? What does anyone brought up before Christianity or out of reach of the Christian message today know of the truth of God? The Bible has a very simple answer. Everyone, everywhere knows–or ought to know–two things: that there is a Creator worthy of adoration and that other creatures should be treated with compassion. We are here back to Jesus' twin-criterion, discussed in chapter 11: love God and love your neighbour. This is not something one can know only by hearing it from Jesus. Rather, this is what you might call a "universal imperative" built into the fabric of creation. It bears down on every man and woman, regardless of cultural context. In his lengthy discussion of God's judgement the apostle Paul in his letter to the Romans makes precisely these points. Men and woman "know" that God deserves thanks and praise:

> For since the creation of the world God's invisible quali-ties–his eternal power and divine nature–have been clearly seen, being understood from what has been made, so that people are without excuse. For although they knew God, they neither glorified him as God nor gave thanks to him (Romans 1:20–21).

Toward the end of this same discussion Paul turns to what men and women (regardless of religion or culture) "know" about how we ought to treat one another:

> They have become filled with every kind of wickedness, evil, greed and depravity. They are full of envy, murder, strife, deceit and malice. They are gossips, slanderers, God-haters, insolent, arrogant and boastful; they invent ways of doing evil; they disobey their parents; they have no understanding, no fidelity, no love, no mercy. Although they know God's righteous decree that those who do such things deserve death, they not only continue to do these very things but also approve of those who practice them (Romans 1:29–32).

The point here is that God will not judge people on the basis of something they do not know–the message of Jesus–but on the basis of the thing they do know: the obligation to adore the Creator and love other creatures. If this is true, suddenly God's judgement is totally fair. Our Afghani woman knows to love God and she knows to love other people: her judgement will focus on precisely these twin obligations. In theory, I can imagine someone who, though having never heard the gospel, looks at the physical world and at the human family and responds with reverence for the Maker and compassion toward others. This would be a sign of true faith, and of the work of the Holy Spirit within them. Such a person would be "safe" on the day of judgement – in theory.

The real question is: does this happen? Romans 1 is very pessimistic: "although they knew God, they neither glorified him as God nor gave thanks to him" and "Although they know God's righteous decree that those who do such things deserve death, they ... continue to do these very things." My great fear is that the utter fairness of God's judgement still leaves us – whether we live in Orūzgān or Oregon – in great need of divine mercy.

I don't doubt that God could, as a sheer act of his mercy, choose to forgive the failures of our hypothetical woman in Afghanistan, regardless of whether she knew about Jesus. I also believe it is legitimate to *hope* that this is so. But if it is, I also have no doubt that this mercy will be given not on the basis of her sincerity or merit but on the grounds of the atonement secured through Jesus' death (discussed in the next few chapters). Whatever the case, I never want to downplay the clear teaching of the Bible (and of Jesus) that God's judgement, however and on whomever it falls, will be entirely fair.

PART 5

CROSS EXAMINATION

Jesus' Death as the Source of Life

**A BRIEF HISTORY OF
CRUCIFIXION**

AT THE HEART OF CHRISTIANITY IS THE SYMBOL OF A CROSS – IN ART,
architecture and even jewelry. We've grown used to the image.
For millions around the world it represents love, hope and comfort – which is strange considering it started out as an instrument
of death.

Years ago, Prof Martin Hengel of the University of Tübin-
gen wrote the definitive volume on this topic, *Crucifixion: In the
Ancient World and the Folly of the Message of the Cross*.[1] He
showed how in ancient times it was widely regarded as the most
brutal and feared form of execution. Of the three official *summa
supplicia*, "ultimate punishments" – crucifixion, decapitation and
burning alive – crucifixion was deemed the supreme penalty.[2] The
Romans had not invented the torture (they probably received it
from the Carthaginians who in turn got it from the Persians[3]),
but they used it to great effect against all manner of serious criminals – military deserters, imperial traitors and bandits. It was

The streets of
Old Jerusalem
where Jesus
was led to his
crucifixion

especially applied to offenders from the slave class, the ancient world's non-persons. Roman citizens, on the other hand, were usually exempt.[4]

Before Emperor Constantine abolished crucifixion in the fourth century, the practice was very common throughout the ancient world. In 4 BC Varus, the governor of Syria, is reported to have crucified 2,000 men after a rebellion against Roman rule.[5] The armies of General Titus (soon to be Emperor Titus) did the same thing in the final weeks of the Jewish war with Rome in AD 70. Having surrounded Jerusalem they started to crucify 500 Jews a day, stationing the crosses in full view of the city walls: "The soldiers out of rage and hatred amused themselves by nailing their prisoners in different postures," writes Josephus in the first century, "and so great was their number, that space could not be found for the crosses nor crosses for the bodies."[6] The Jews themselves were not above using this form of torture either. A century and a half earlier Alexander Jannaeus, the ruler and high priest in Jerusalem, crucified 800 rebel Pharisees in full view of their wives and children. As the men hung there slowly dying, their families were slaughtered in front of them.[7]

The main reason for this widespread use of crucifixion, Martin Hengel notes, was its "supreme efficacy as a deterrent."[8] Death was slow, public and exceedingly painful. It sent a very powerful message. Although there was no "correct" method of crucifixion, victims were frequently scourged beforehand, enhancing the appearance (and reality) of brutalisation. After being stripped naked they were usually taken to a visible place, often a hill, and fastened to a large wooden beam. Sometimes a simple vertical pole was used. Other times a cross-beam was affixed creating the figure we usually associate with Jesus' death. Victims could be tied with ropes to the cross but nails were the strong preference. There is even a report from the first-century Roman philosopher Seneca that victims were also occasionally impaled through the genitals.[9] No wonder he writes on another occasion: "Can any man be found willing to be fastened to the accursed tree ... drawing the breath of life amid long-drawn-out agony? He would have many excuses for dying even before mounting the cross."[10] Crucifixion, in other words, was the last death a man would choose.

WHY THE SCANT ARCHAELOGICAL EVIDENCE?

Despite the plethora of written accounts of crucifixion from the ancient world, so far only one piece of archaeological evidence has been uncovered. In 1968 Israeli archaeologists discovered a tomb just north of Jerusalem in which were found some Jewish burial boxes (ossuaries). One of them was inscribed "Jehohanan and Jehohanan ben Jehohanan," meaning that the box contained the bones of a father and his son of the same name. Analysis of the bones revealed the remains of a male right-heel bone that had been pierced through by an iron nail 11.5 cm long and so badly bent it had never been removed from the foot. A plaque of wood from an olive tree was still attached. It was a remarkable find and has taught us quite a bit about the method of crucifixion.[11]

That we have found only one piece of archaeological evidence for crucifixion is not as odd as it might seem. Crucifixion victims were usually not granted a proper burial but typically left to the wild animals and birds of prey or else thrown onto the rubbish heap; the dishonour of crucifixion did not end with the final breath.[12] Having said that, the example of Jehohanan shows that some victims *were* given a burial. Jews had quite strict burial customs, as the first-century writer Josephus makes clear: "the Jews are so careful about funeral rites that even malefactors who have been sentenced to crucifixion are taken down and buried before sunset."[13] Jesus was likewise saved from the horrible end usually reserved for the crucified. He was properly buried.[14]

It is hard to comprehend, then, how disturbing the modern use of the cross as a holy symbol would have seemed to people in the first century. And the idea of wearing it as a necklace – as a piece of fashion – would have been considered macabre. It would be like one of us walking around with a replica of an electric chair around our neck.

But the first Christians seem to have revelled in the awful death of Jesus. The cross was the centre of their rituals, ethics and belief. Even today, pilgrims to Jerusalem walk the *via dolorosa* – the "way of pain" – Jesus' path to the cross. The evidence that the Via Dolorosa was the actual path Jesus travelled to his crucifixion is not very good – non-existent actually. But that he was crucified somewhere in the city of Jerusalem around the year

30 is beyond dispute. Even the most sceptical of contemporary scholars, such as Prof John Dominic Crossan of De Paul University, "take it absolutely for granted that Jesus was crucified under Pontius Pilate." He continues, "Security about the *fact* of the crucifixion derives not only from the unlikelihood that Christians would have invented it but also from the existence of two early and independent non-Christian witnesses to it."[15] He is talking here about the Roman writer Tacitus and the Jewish writer Josephus (discussed in chapter 3). The straightforward words of Josephus are worth recalling: "Pilate, upon hearing him accused by men of the highest standing amongst us, had condemned him to be crucified."[16] Thus, even popular naysayers not bound by the constraints of historical method know not to attempt a rewrite of this immovable historical fact. "The reality is," writes Bishop John Shelby Spong in a moment of good sense, "that Jesus was executed by the Romans. The reality is that the common method of execution by the Romans was crucifixion."[17]

WHO WITNESSED THE CRUCIFIXION?

In one of Bishop Spong's less careful statements he says that "no one was there either to witness the death of Jesus or to record it."[18] Hence, no details about the crucifixion can be known. It is true that the Gospels speak of disciples fleeing when Jesus was arrested[19] but the very same Gospels say that others of his followers did not flee.[20]

It might be interesting here to look more closely at what we know of eyewitnesses in biblical accounts. Prof Richard Bauckham of the University of St Andrews (Scotland) has recently argued that the unknown individuals explicitly named in other events in the Gospels are likely to be the very sources of those stories themselves: a blind man named Bartimaeus,[21] a synagogue leader called Jairus[22] and many others. There seems to be no other explanation for why some people are named and others are not, especially when we consider that the tendency in the three related Gospels (Matthew, Mark and Luke) was to drop names, not add them. In other words, it doesn't at all look like there was an effort in early Christianity to invent names and place them into the story of Jesus for credibility. The opposite was true.

Perhaps the most significant group of named eyewitnesses of the Passion is the women disciples. It is a surprisingly male perspective that says *all* of the disciples fled. Here, all four Gospels are in basic agreement with Mark's Gospel:

> Some women were watching from a distance. Among them were Mary Magdalene, Mary the mother of James the younger and of Joseph, and Salome. In Galilee these women had followed him and cared for his needs. Many other women who had come up with him to Jerusalem were also there (Mark 15:40–41; also Matthew 27:55–56, Luke 23:49; John 19:25–27).

Drawing on Richard Bauckham's insights, we have here another indication of an eyewitness source–indeed, several eyewitness sources–right at the crucial point of Jesus' death. Only the most dogmatic kind of scepticism would dare suggest these names were added for effect. In first-century Palestine the testimony of women was deeply distrusted (by men).[23] If this were a historical prop on the part of all four Gospel writers, it is not a very good one. Not until the middle of the twentieth century, when women gained full equality before the law, would it ever have entered a person's head that women could be added to a historical narrative to enhance its credibility![24] No, what we have here is a simple statement of fact that the women who had supported Jesus in Galilee stood by him–albeit "from a distance"–to the very end. They therefore probably played a decisive role in shaping this most famous of ancient narratives. As James Dunn observes, "the only eyewitnesses that all the Evangelists agree on were women disciples.... There is a strong possibility, therefore, that these women played a significant role in forming the tradition of Jesus' death."[25] The Christian church–and the world at large–is forever in their debt.

CHAPTER 15

THE REASONS FOR JESUS' DEATH

WHY DID JESUS DIE? OF COURSE, CHRISTIAN BELIEVERS HAVE THE ready answer: "He died for our sins." But historians usually mean something different when they ask this question. They are looking for the cultural and political factors that could lead this preacher and healer from Nazareth to end his life on a Roman cross.

It is a vital question and one that should fit with our total picture of the historical Jesus. As James Dunn quips, "To be 'historical' the historical Jesus must have been crucifiable."[1] In other words, any portrait of Jesus' life that leaves us scratching our heads wondering why on earth Jewish and Roman authorities would want him dead has probably missed the mark. A Jesus who simply wanted to see equality and justice for all, without any radical vision of God's in-breaking kingdom, is hardly likely to have provoked the ire of the high priest in Jerusalem, let alone that of the Roman prefect Pontius Pilate. Unless we can draw some pretty straight lines between his career as a teacher and healer and his death on a Roman cross, we have probably not grasped the real Jesus.

Temple model
in Jerusalem

So, why did Jesus die? What factors contributed to such a brutal climax to his ministry?

BUILDING TENSION

The first thing to note is that Jesus was associated from the beginning with a first-century Jewish movement whose prophet-like leader, John the Baptist, was himself executed by the Rome-appointed Herod Antipas. The Gospels of Mark and Matthew attribute the death of John the Baptist to his uncompromising proclamation of God's requirements – he had a bit to say about Herod's relationship with his brother's wife.[2] Our Jewish source, Josephus, indicates that Antipas was equally alarmed by John's apparent sway over the masses: "Herod decided therefore that it would be much better to strike first and be rid of him before his work led to an uprising."[3] As mentioned earlier, the Baptist was probably something of a mentor to the early Jesus – they shared the same vision of God's impending judgement and the same call, marked by baptism, to radical renewal. John's fate must have hung over Jesus like a bad omen.

Second, it is clear that Jesus had some significant clashes with the religious authorities, particularly with the Pharisees, from quite early on in his career. Perhaps the most serious were his friendships with "sinners," especially the way he directly offered them forgiveness of sins, and his baffling deeds, which some of the religious elite attributed to the power of Satan (as we saw in chapter 9). This was no small charge. Joachim Jeremias pointed out years ago that black magic, which in effect is what Jesus was accused of, was one of the religious crimes punishable by stoning.[4] It is unlikely anyone was actually calling for Jesus' death early on in his career, but these unofficial rumours of sorcery and constant clashes with Pharisees must have created an atmosphere of great tension around the Jesus movement.

But Jesus' ministry of preaching and healing, as confrontational as it was, cannot have been the ultimate cause of his downfall. One clear indication of this, often noted by scholars, is that Jesus' main antagonists during these Galilean years, the Pharisees, play little role in his arrest and trial. It is the priests, the temple elite, who spring into action against Jesus at the end.[5] This tells us that what finally brought Jesus down was not some theological disagreement with rival Jewish teachers but his confrontation with the true power base of Israel's national life, the priestly aristocracy. This leads us in one direction.

JESUS VERSUS THE TEMPLE

Virtually everyone writing on the topic today agrees that the immediate cause of Jesus' arrest and execution was the events of his final week when he came to Jerusalem for the Passover festival.

Jews believed that Jerusalem, and the temple that stood there, was the dwelling place of God. God ruled all the world, but he touched the earth in a special way at just this point. The feeling about this city then was not just cultural; it was profoundly spiritual. Adding to expectations was a passage in the Jewish Scriptures that foretold of the Messiah entering the holy city on a donkey: "Shout, Daughter Jerusalem!" wrote the prophet Zechariah, "your king comes to you, righteous and having salvation, lowly and riding on a donkey" (Zechariah 9:9). The prophecy was well known, and Jesus used it to make a very public statement to the huge crowds in Jerusalem for Passover, in what is traditionally called his triumphal entry (celebrated these days as Palm Sunday):

> As Jesus neared Bethphage and Bethany, at the place
> called the Mount of Olives, he sent out two of the disciples,
> saying, "Go into the town opposite. As you enter, you will
> find a colt tied up there on which no-one has ever ridden.
> Untie it and bring it here.... They brought the colt to Jesus,
> threw their cloaks over it and got Jesus to sit on it.... Now
> as he neared the place where the road descends the Mount
> of Olives, the whole crowd of disciples began to praise God
> joyfully and loudly, "Blessed be the king who comes in the
> name of the Lord!" (Luke 19:29–38).

This was more than a simple "three cheers for Jesus." It was the moment the teacher from Nazareth finally went public with the suggestion that he was some kind of king. For those who loved Jesus, it must have been spine-tingling stuff. For those who didn't, it was alarming. And so Prof Paula Fredriksen of Boston University is probably correct when she says:

A straight line connects the Triumphal Entry and the Crucifixion. A pilgrim crowd noisily proclaiming the coming of
the Kingdom, not to mention the coming of their King, would
certainly provoke Pilate's attention and concern: With much
less provocation, he had swung into bloody action before.[6]

But Jesus didn't stop with this not-so-subtle hint about his
status. He entered the temple itself and, in the middle of the
sacred precinct, created a dazzling disturbance. Each Passover,
the priests allowed a live-stock "supermarket" in the temple area
so people could buy sacrifices for the festival. It was potentially
very lucrative and exploitative. Jesus was outraged. All four Gospels record him driving out the buyers and sellers, and throwing
over the tables of the bankers.

> Then he entered the temple area and began driving out
> those who were selling. "It is written," he said to them,
> " 'My house will be a house of prayer'; but you have made it
> 'a den of robbers.' " Every day he was teaching at the temple.
> But the chief priests, the teachers of the law and the leaders
> among the people were trying to kill him. Yet they could
> not find any way to do it, because all the people hung on his
> words (Luke 19:45 – 48).

The temple precinct was 300m long and 500m wide. Twelve
football fields would fit into its area. And Jesus stood there and
accused the temple authorities of turning God's house into a "den
of robbers."

Traditionally, this episode is known as the cleansing of the
temple, but it was more than a cleansing. Most experts believe
it was a sign of doom. By overturning the tables of the priestly
bankers Jesus was signalling God's overthrow of the temple itself.
Occasionally, Jesus was explicit about the end of the temple:

> When some were speaking about how the temple had
> been adorned with beautiful stones, Jesus said, "These
> stones you are looking at–days are coming when not one
> stone will be left on another; they will all be torn down"
> (Luke 21:5 – 6).

Within a generation, this came true. Palestine was embroiled in a full-scale uprising against Rome. The Romans responded with massive force. In August AD 70 they stormed Jerusalem and razed the temple to the ground. Josephus, an eyewitness to much of the war, describes the final moments: "While the temple blazed, the victors plundered everything.... The roar of the flames streaming far and wide mingled with the groans of the falling victims." Whether you view it as divine foresight or a lucky guess, Jesus' words and actions against the temple were eerily fulfilled within living memory. But before Jerusalem burned, Jesus of course faced his own catastrophe and, according to most experts, this public protest against the temple was the match that lit the fuse. As Ed Sanders once put it: "The gun may already have been cocked, but it was the temple demonstration which pulled the trigger."[7]

An incident in the temple some thirty years later provides a striking historical parallel to this conclusion. The Jewish historian Josephus records how a certain "Jesus son of Ananias" suddenly appeared in the temple courts four years before the outbreak of the war with Rome (so around AD 62) crying out, "A voice from the east, a voice from the west, a voice from the four winds; a voice against Jerusalem and the sanctuary." He took his message throughout the streets and alleys of the Holy City. People were incensed. Leading citizens abused and assaulted him. On one occasion he was even arrested by the Jewish authorities and taken to the Roman governor Albinus. Josephus continues:

> There, although flayed to the bone with scourges, he neither sued for mercy nor shed a tear, but, merely introducing the most mournful of variations into his ejaculation, responded with "Woe to Jerusalem!" When Albinus, the governor, asked him who and whence he was and why he uttered these cries, he answered him never a word, but unceasingly reiterated his dirge over the city, until Albinus pronounced him a maniac and let him go.[8]

Jesus son of Ananias apparently continued his prophetic lament against the temple until someone hurled a stone at him and killed him on the spot. It was not long, however, as even Josephus notes, before his portent was proved right.

Three decades earlier another prophet made similar threats against Jerusalem and its temple but, whereas the son of Ananias could be dismissed as lone madman, Jesus son of Joseph had a significant following and a history of flouting purity rules. What's more, he had dared to perform a prophet-like sign in the temple, temporarily disrupting the exchange of sacred coinage and forbidding the sale of sacrificial animals. He too was arrested by the leading citizens and taken to the Roman governor. He too was beaten and scourged. But this man could not be released. In the minds of the authorities his threat was too great, especially at a religiously charged time like the Passover festival. The well-known trouble-maker from Galilee had to be killed, not just beaten and scourged. His two prophetic signs—a royal entry into Jerusalem and the overturning of the priestly tables—amounted to a claim that authority to rule God's people rested not on the Jerusalem elite but on the man on the donkey, the man who dared to challenge the temple itself.

JESUS AS THE TEMPLE

In some ways, Jesus' view was similar to that of the Essenes at Qumran who also believed that God would establish an ideal temple (with them as its leaders).[9] But whereas the Essenes took their protest out into the desert, Jesus took his right into the temple courts. And whereas the Essenes speculated in meticulous detail about the dimensions and functions of the new temple,[10] Jesus appears to have left this question open. There is certainly no indication that he thought of himself or his disciples as the replacement priesthood (as the Essenes apparently did). Far from it, Jesus' offer of divine forgiveness *independent of all temple rituals* suggests that he, like John the Baptist, believed that the emergency in Israel was so great that the ordinary means of atonement (sacrifice in the temple) was insufficient to avert the wrath of God; something completely new was needed. But what?

As we will see in the next chapter, Jesus believed that his death on the cross—his shed blood at Passover time—played a decisive role in the forgiveness and renewal of God's people. This, combined with the vagueness of his teaching about what would replace the temple, invites the very striking interpretation of Jesus' threat against the temple found in the Gospel of John:

The Jews then responded to him, "What sign can you show us to prove your authority to do all this?" Jesus answered them, "Destroy this temple, and I will raise it again in three days." They replied, "It has taken forty-six years to build this temple, and you are going to raise it in three days?" But the temple he had spoken of was his body (John 2:18–21).

For John, the crucified and raised Jesus replaced the temple; he was the new locus of God's presence and mercy. Believing in him brought one near to God and removed one's sins, just as the temple had once done.[11] Here's an interesting thought: it was Jesus' public criticism of the temple that triggered his arrest and execution; and it was his execution that brought the forgiveness that made the temple redundant.

In any case, the main point for now is that Jesus' threat against the temple (and implicit claim to an authority superior to that of the temple) moved the priestly aristocracy to act against him. The fact that this threat came immediately after entering Jerusalem on a donkey in royal style gave the authorities a pretext for handing Jesus over to the Roman governor as a rebel with pretensions to kingship.[12] The priests no doubt knew that Jesus was not a military threat; Pontius Pilate must have known that he commanded no army. But good order was the first concern for such leaders, and anyone stirring up the crowds with claims of authority and talk of a coming kingdom threatened that order, especially at Passover time.[13] Killing one man to avert even the remotest possibility of an uprising was a very small thing to a man such as Pilate. He had done it before and would do so again. A contemporary of Pilate, Philo of Alexandria, listed the litany of Pilate's crimes while governing Judaea: "the briberies, the insults, the robberies, the outrages and wanton injuries, the executions without trial constantly repeated, the ceaseless and supremely grievous cruelty."[14] Jesus of Nazareth was one of many who fell foul of the Roman governor and the Jerusalem elite. It is only the *meaning* attached to his crucifixion that makes this death, among the countless thousands of others from the period, a topic of intense interest two millennia later. It is to the meaning of Jesus' death that I want to turn in the next chapter.

CHAPTER 16

JESUS' VIEW OF HIS DEATH

HISTORY IS FULL OF PROMINENT PEOPLE WHOSE DEATHS CAME AS a shock. Leaders of great vision such as John F. Kennedy – lost in an instant. Artists like John Lennon who inspired a generation – killed in a moment of madness. Celebrities like Princess Diana – taken in the prime of life. By contrast, Jesus seems to have known where his bold career would take him.

Jesus knew full well that some of Israel's most famous prophets had been killed. And his own mentor, John the Baptist, was

Inside the
Garden Tomb
in Jerusalem

beheaded just a couple of years earlier during a party for Herod Antipas, the ruler of Galilee.

The clearest evidence that Jesus knew his destiny comes in a statement recorded in three independent sources. During the Passover festival of AD 30, as he sat down for his Last Supper, he spoke words that would be repeated every week in churches throughout the world.

> Jesus took a loaf of bread, gave thanks for it, broke it and gave it to them saying, "This is my body which is given for you; do this in remembrance of me." And in the same way, after eating the meal, he took the cup of wine and said, "This cup is the new covenant in my blood, which is poured out for you" (Luke 22:19–20).

Jesus anticipated his death. So what? So did Martin Luther King, Mahatma Ghandi and a host of other controversial religious and political leaders through history. The more tantalizing question is: What was the significance of his suffering? Here, we come face to face with one of the most powerful and enduring themes in Western thought, a theme captured on countless war memorials and gravestones of fallen soldiers: "Greater love hath no man than this, that a man lay down his life for his friends."[1] From the very beginning Jesus has been seen as the very epitome of self-sacrifice. But what was it for? He was not defending a nation or trying to bring down a tyrant. Why such sacrifice?

I want to answer this question in two parts. Before turning to the viewpoint of Jesus himself, I want to start with the earliest *Christian* understanding of Jesus' death; that is, the interpretation offered by his immediate followers. Here the historian is blessed—if that's the right word—with amazingly early and clear evidence.

"CHRIST DIED FOR OUR SINS": THE EARLIEST CREED

There is a paragraph in Paul's first letter to the Corinthians (15:3–5) that scholars date to the first years or even months of the Christian movement. Paul's letter itself can be dated to about AD 55 (predating the earliest Gospel by a decade), but it is a small quotation within the letter that is the focus of so much scholarly attention. Toward the end of this epistle Paul pauses to recall for his readers a formal summary of the faith – a creed – that he passed on to them when they first heard the Christian gospel five years earlier, AD 50. This was a strongly Jewish practice. Many such teachers crafted memorable summaries of their message so that disciples could recall and rehearse the fundamentals without deviation; in an aural culture, memorization of fixed material was par for the course. Entire books have been written on this subject and its relevance to early Christianity.[2]

Interestingly, Paul admits that he was not the composer of the creed. He received it from others when he first became a disciple: "For what I received I passed on to you as of first importance ..." (here Paul uses the technical jargon for delivering fixed oral tradition).[3] Unless Paul is simply lying to his converts, this immediately pushes us back into the AD 30s when Paul began his ministry. There is debate about whether Paul "received" this creed in AD 33/34 when he spent a fortnight in Jerusalem with the apostle Peter and James the brother of Jesus, or two years earlier in AD 31/32 at the time of his conversion in Damascus.[4] Either way, James Dunn puts it bluntly: "This tradition, we can be entirely confident, was formulated as tradition within months of Jesus' death."[5] Let me quote the creed, this tradition, which was passed on to the apostle Paul himself "as of first importance":

> that Christ died for our sins according to the Scriptures,
> that he was buried, that he was raised on the third day
> according to the Scriptures, and that he appeared to Cephas,
> and then to the Twelve (1 Corinthians 15:3–5).

The significance of this creed is obvious because it establishes beyond doubt that the core of the Jesus story – his status as "Christ," his death, burial, claimed resurrection and appearances and founding of a famous Twelve – was not part of a slowly developing legend. Already by the mid–30s AD this story was sufficiently well known to become part of a formal teaching summary memorised by disciples far and wide. The notion sometimes put forward that Jesus' role as Christ and Saviour was only developed much later (some even suggest by fourth-century Emperor Constantine) is untenable from a historian's perspective. This early creed, among numerous other pieces of evidence, makes clear that all of the major ideas of the Christian faith were developed–if that's even the right word–in the very first generation of Jesus' followers.

We will look again at this creed when we discuss Jesus' resurrection. For now, I just want us to focus on the opening phrase: "Christ died for our sins according to the Scriptures." This tells the historian at least two things. First, within a few years of the crucifixion the leading disciples–the only ones with authority to compose a creed like this–were interpreting Jesus' death as a sacrifice *for sins*. Second, this interpretation was believed to be "according to the Scriptures," that is, in accordance with and foretold by the Jewish Scriptures or Old Testament. So, where in the Old Testament do we learn about a death for sins?

At the very heart of the religion of the Old Testament was the notion of sacrifice for sins. The passages are too numerous to list, but the following text, from the book of Leviticus, the fourth book of the Jewish Bible, describes the central annual event of Yom Kippur, the Day of Atonement:

> He [the high priest] shall then slaughter the goat for the sin offering for the people and take its blood behind the curtain and do with it as he did with the bull's blood: He shall sprinkle it on the atonement cover and in front of it. In this way he will make atonement for the Most Holy Place because of the uncleanness and rebellion of the Israelites, whatever their sins have been (Leviticus 16:15–16).

The notion of "blood sacrifice" or "atonement" was very, very common in antiquity. Although there is a tendency today to condemn the practice as barbaric and bloodthirsty, there is no avoiding the historical reality that ancient cultures, both Eastern and Western, saw in it a powerful symbol of both justice and renewal. Blood is the stuff of life and was thought to belong to the divinity, the source of life, not to humanity. Hence, it could be offered to the deity to make peace between the creature and the god. Ideas of blood atonement are found not only amongst the Jews but also throughout the Graeco-Roman religions and even the sacred texts of Hinduism.[6] Islam, on the other hand, repudiates the notion of atoning sacrifice, not because it is bloodthirsty (the sacrifice of sheep during the pilgrimage to Mecca is a central rite of the festival) but because, as the Quran itself states, "Every soul is accountable for what evil it commits, and no soul shall bear the burden of another soul."[7] In other words, no one else can atone for your wrongdoing. You bear your own responsibility before God. In Islam you atone for your own sins through practising alms-giving, prayer and so on.[8]

None of this is to suggest that the Jewish notion of atonement is exactly the same as that of ancient pagan religion. Far from it. The most striking difference is that, whereas in Graeco-Roman practice offering a sacrifice was a kind of emergency measure performed by men in the hope of appeasing an otherwise harmful and unpredictable deity, atonement in Judaism is seen as the gift of a merciful God who delights in withholding his judgement from his people, despite their sins.

Returning to my point, when the early Christian creed says that Christ died for our sins "according to the Scriptures" it is deliberately setting what happened to Jesus in the context of Jewish atonement theology. But a number of leading scholars insist we can say more. They point to a very strange passage in the Old Testament, written centuries before Christ, that speaks of a mysterious "servant" of the Lord who would suffer and die in the manner of the sacrificial animal.[9] His death would be "for our sins." It comes in the book of Isaiah:

> He had no beauty or majesty to attract us to him,
>   nothing in his appearance that we should desire him.
> He was despised and rejected by others,
>   a man of suffering, and familiar with pain.
> Like one from whom people hide their faces
>   he was despised, and we held him in low esteem.
> Surely he took up our pain
>   and bore our suffering,
> yet we considered him punished by God,
>   stricken by him, and afflicted.
> But he was pierced for our transgressions,
>   he was crushed for our iniquities;
> the punishment that brought us peace was on him,
>   and by his wounds we are healed.
> We all, like sheep, have gone astray,

each of us has turned to our own way;
and the LORD has laid on him
the iniquity of us all (Isaiah 53:2–6).

This passage makes it immediately comprehensible not only that the first Christians would interpret their Lord's death through the lens of Isaiah 53 but also that Jesus himself would do so.

THE PASSOVER

In addition to the general notion of Old Testament sacrifice and the specific prophecy of Isaiah 53, Jesus' words at the Last Supper point us to another important element of the Jewish Scriptures: "This is my body which is given for you.... This cup is the new covenant in my blood, which is poured out for you" (Luke 22:19–20). Jesus was speaking near the time of the Passover when tens of thousands of Jews flooded the Holy City and the temple. His words indicated not only that he would die but why.

Any mention of "blood poured out" at this time would have reminded Jews of the Passover sacrifice. Passover recalled the Israelites' deliverance from slavery in Egypt centuries earlier. On that occasion their ancestors had daubed the doorposts of their homes with the blood of a lamb to protect them. When God's judgement fell on Egypt that night it "passed over" those houses with blood on them.

In Jesus' day the Passover was still celebrated with the killing and eating of a lamb. The lamb was killed in the Jerusalem temple and its blood was "poured out" at the altar. It was a sacrifice to the Lord, a symbol that God's judgement will "pass over" his beloved people because it had fallen on another (the lamb).

Understanding all of this clarifies Jesus' strange words at the Last Supper. Jesus frequently warned of God's judgement on those who refused the path of love. But by referring to his coming death as the "new covenant in his blood ... poured out for others" he was teaching that his personal sacrifice would save people from divine judgement. He was the ultimate Passover Lamb, the means of receiving God's forgiveness rather than judgement.

This interpretation is confirmed by the reference to a "new covenant." These words lead us to just one passage in the Jewish Scriptures that can provide the background. The prophet Jeremiah promised that after the breaking of the first covenant (the one ratified by Moses), God would establish a new one:

> "The days are coming," declares the LORD, "when I will make a new covenant with the house of Israel and with the house of Judah. It will not be like the covenant I made with their ancestors when I took them by the hand to lead them out of Egypt, because they broke my covenant, though I was a husband to them," declares the LORD. "This is the covenant I will make with the house of Israel after that time," declares the LORD. "I will put my law in their minds and write it on their hearts. I will be their God, and they will be my people. No longer will they teach their neighbours, or say to one another, 'Know the LORD,' because they will all know me, from the least of them to the greatest," declares the LORD. "For I will forgive their wickedness and will remember their sins no more" (Jeremiah 31:31–34).

According to Jeremiah, the new agreement or covenant would internalise God's law, writing it on the human heart, and it would wipe the slate clean through the forgiveness of sins. (This sounds a lot like the leading themes of Jesus' entire ministry.) This must be the covenant Jesus believed would be ratified through his shed blood. It was a sacrifice for the forgiveness of sins.

THE DISTURBING IDEA OF ATONEMENT

The idea that God requires a blood sacrifice is a disturbing one for many today. But it wasn't for an ancient Jew like Jesus. The God of Israel was perfectly just. He loved his people, but he couldn't simply forgive them. Just as a judge wouldn't release a criminal simply because he was positively inclined toward him, so God will not forgive the guilty without exacting payment. Love it or hate it, that was the Jewish point of view. And Jesus literally embodied the thought. His death would satisfy God's justice and so secure God's mercy.

It is surprising to me, as an historian as much as a Christian, that the prominent British minister and writer, Steve Chalke, could criticize the ancient notion of atoning sacrifice in favour of seeing Jesus' death essentially as a loving identification with the powerless (his book itself is a wonderful call for Christians to identify with the poor and oppressed):

> How then have we come to believe that at the cross this God of love suddenly decides to vent his anger and wrath on his own Son? The fact is that the cross isn't a form of cosmic child abuse – a vengeful Father, punishing his Son for an offence he has not even committed. Understandably, both people inside and outside of the Church have found this twisted version of events morally dubious and a huge barrier to faith. Deeper than that, however, is that such a concept stands in total contradiction to the statement "God is love." If the cross is a personal act of violence perpetrated by God towards humankind but borne by his Son, then it makes a mockery of Jesus' own teaching to love your enemies and to refuse to repay evil with evil. The truth is, the cross is a symbol of love. It is a demonstration of just how far God as Father and Jesus as his Son are prepared to go to prove that love. The cross is a vivid statement of the powerlessness of love.[10]

There is an obvious straw man here – what Christian has ever thought of atonement as "cosmic child abuse"! The statement also reads like an attempt to rewrite the New Testament understanding of Jesus' death in light of the modern aversion to retributive justice, i.e. the notion that the wrong-doer deserves punishment regardless of the penalty's restorative effects or usefulness as a deterrent. I will leave it to others to offer theological and philosophical comment on these matters. My concern is historical. Chalke can only write what he does by overlooking the widespread notion in antiquity, cherished by Jews as well as Christians, that the God of love and justice pardons his people *through sacrificial atonement*. The historical Jesus never pitted divine love against divine judgement. Both themes stand side by side in the Gospels (as we have seen throughout), just as they stand side by side in the Jewish concept of atonement. God forgives the beloved as he condemns the substitute. We might not warm to the idea, but we cannot wave a wand and remove it from our sources.

Christianity teaches that Jesus' death on the cross was a kind of payment for sin – it was the price of justice, so to speak. None of us could respect a judge who simply let a lawbreaker off the hook. In the same way God can't simply ignore sin and still be considered perfect and just. So Jesus, whom Christians teach is himself divine, willingly pays that price. It is a sign of how much God wants us, and the price he was willing to pay to deal with the corruption of the world and humanity.

Something that helps me understand this is to imagine a judge who, once he has justly passed sentence, instead of condemning the lawbreaker, gets out of his seat and pays the fine himself. The Bible tells us that Jesus is the one who judges sin, so the comparison makes sense. It is not God forcing Jesus to do it. It is Jesus the Lord and Judge, the embodiment of God, doing it himself.

It can be moral for one person to pay the penalty on behalf of another, if he isn't coerced into it. The Bible is clear that Jesus died willingly–it was his mission to fulfill the new covenant. Furthermore, the striking teaching of the New Testament is that "God was reconciling the world to himself in Christ" (2 Corinthians 5:19). In other words, God himself was absorbing the price of judgement. God was making sure that sin was dealt with, the price of justice was paid–and he was paying it himself. He wasn't punishing a third, uninvolved party when Jesus died for sins. This is why Chalke's "cosmic child abuse" reference is so wide of the mark.

Of course, in historical terms, Jesus was killed by Romans who wanted to keep the peace with the religious authorities of the day. God didn't literally kill Jesus. But we are talking about the spiritual meaning of Jesus' death. Spiritually, it is an act of love from God so that imperfect people can be perfectly acceptable to the perfect God.

And all of these themes come to a beautiful climax in the crucifixion scene itself when, according to Luke's Gospel, one of the criminals crucified alongside Jesus that day found the mercy for which Jesus was dying:

> Two others who were criminals were also led out with him to be executed. And when they arrived at the place called "The Skull," they crucified him there along with the criminals–one on Jesus' right, the other on his left. And the soldiers divided his clothing by placing bets; and the people stood by, watching. The leaders even made fun of him, saying, "He rescued others, let him rescue himself if he really is

God's Christ, his Chosen One." The soldiers also ridiculed him, coming up and offering him bitter wine. They said, "If you really are the King of the Jews, rescue yourself." There was a placard above him which read: THIS IS THE KING OF THE JEWS. One of the criminals who hung there was abusing Jesus, saying, "Aren't you supposed to be the Christ? Rescue yourself and us."

But the other criminal responded with a rebuke: "Have you no fear of God? After all, you are under the same death sentence. Yet, we are here justly; we are receiving what we deserve for our actions, but he has done nothing wrong." Then he said, "Jesus, please remember me when you come into your kingdom." And Jesus replied, "I tell you the truth, today you will be with me in Paradise."

By this time, it was already about midday, but darkness came over the whole land until three in the afternoon, because the sun stopped shining. The curtain of the Temple was torn down the middle. Then Jesus cried out in a loud voice, "Father, into your hands I entrust my spirit!" With these words he breathed his last breath (Luke 23:32–46).

There were countless crucifixions in the first century. Indeed, as I said earlier, in the final stages of the war in August AD 70 the Romans crucified 500 Jews a day outside Jerusalem's walls. So, at one level, what happened to Jesus was not unique—many people met a similar fate. But when you consider the meaning Jesus attached to his cross and the impact it has had on countless millions of lives throughout history, beginning with the criminal crucified alongside Jesus, there is a sense in which his was a most extraordinary death. It was the means of God's mercy for the world.

TWO VIEWS OF THE CROSS

I recently had the privilege of visiting a stunning museum on Rome's Palatine Hill, where the emperors once resided. Amid the enormous ruins of the imperial palaces and guardhouses is a modern building packed with statues, inscriptions and frescoes dating from the early days of Rome to the height of the empire. In one of the rooms is a section of wall from a second–third century AD guardhouse. On it is a faint but still legible piece of anti-Christian graffiti. Tourists tend to walk right by it unaware of the potent historical insight it offers into the clash between ancient Rome and the early followers of Jesus. The hastily drawn inscription mocks an otherwise unknown Christian named Alexamenos, who was perhaps incarcerated at the time on the other side of the wall. It depicts his deity as a crucified man with a mule's head (signalling stupidity). Alexamenos himself is drawn to the left of the cross with an arm raised in homage to his dying Lord. Underneath, in very poor Greek–the kind you would expect from a Roman guard–we read the words: *Alexamenos sebete theon*, "Alexamenos worships god." It was a potent insult: the sheer foolishness of worshipping a crucified man.

We see in this graffito the clash of two worldviews. One looked at the crucifixion of Jesus and could only see shame, weakness and failure. The fool Jesus died under the empire's *summum supplicium*, ultimate penalty. This Roman viewpoint has its modern counterpart, I think, in the charge of Richard Dawkins that the very notion of Jesus' atoning death is vicious, repellent and barking mad![11] But as I stood there in front of the graffito and ran my hands across its mocking inscription, I could not help thinking of Alexamenos on the other side of the wall. He would have seen things very differently from his Roman captors. For him, the death of Jesus was anything but a failure. In the ugliness of crucifixion God had displayed his justice toward sin and, at the same time, his mercy toward sinners. The cross was the means of atonement and the basis of God's new covenant with the world. Alexamenos must have known – as every Christian in antiquity knew – the striking words of Jesus at his Last Supper: "This cup is the new covenant in my blood, which is poured out for you." I like to think that Alexamenos took great comfort in those words, especially if he himself was facing execution, knowing that he was a recipient of God's mercy. Standing in that museum, I have never felt so keenly the ancient and modern significance of Jesus' cross.

PART 6

THE RESURRECTION

How Could It Happen?
What Does It Matter?

JESUS PROBABLY WASN'T THE MOST REVERED TEACHER OF HIS DAY. In the year AD 30 names like Rabbi Hillel or Shammai were almost certainly more recognisable than his. But today Hillel and Shammai are virtually unknown and the name Jesus is revered by millions throughout the world.

Why?

Part of the answer is the fiery missionary zeal of the first Christians. But the spark that lit this fuse was the extraordinary claim that their crucified master had been raised from the dead. This conviction drove them to take his words and deeds to the ends of the earth. We live in the wake of that.

But what can historians say about the resurrection story? More than you might think. Hundreds of scholarly books and articles are devoted to the topic. In universities throughout the world the question is still taken seriously.

Scholars agree that there is an irreducible historical core to the resurrection story that cannot be explained away as pious legend

The Garden Tomb in Jerusalem, a possible location of Jesus' burial

or wholesale deceit. Prof Ed Sanders, who warms a seat at the sceptical end of mainstream scholarship, puts it well: "That Jesus' followers (and later Paul) had resurrection experiences is, in my judgement, a fact. What the reality was that gave rise to the experiences I do not know."[1] This is typical of the secular study of Jesus: something strange happened, we're just not quite sure what!

One very interesting study of the resurrection comes from the late, great Pinchas Lapide, a German scholar of ancient Judaism and Christianity and a practicing Jew. He concluded:

> Concerning the resurrection of Jesus on Easter Sunday, I was for decades a Sadducee [a Jewish sect which denies the afterlife]. I am no longer a Sadducee since the following deliberation has caused me to think this through anew.... [W]hen these peasants, shepherds, and fishermen, who betrayed and denied their master and then failed him miserably, suddenly could be changed overnight into a confident mission society, convinced of salvation and able to work with much more success after Easter than before Easter, then no vision or hallucination is sufficient to explain such a revolutionary transformation.... If the defeated and depressed group of disciples overnight could change into a victorious movement of faith, based only on autosuggestion or self-deception—without a fundamental faith experience—then this would be a much greater miracle than the resurrection itself. In a purely logical analysis, the resurrection of Jesus is "the lesser of two evils" for all those who seek a rational explanation of the worldwide consequences of that Easter faith.[2]

The second half of Lapide's book was an attempt to reconcile the historical judgement that Jesus rose again with his orthodox Jewish perspective that denies Jesus' status as the Messiah. His solution was ingenious: God raised the prophet Jesus in order to launch a heretical movement (Christianity) that would be able, in a way the Jews would never have attempted, to teach the Gentiles at least two core Jewish principles: belief in one God and moral law.

If nothing else, Prof Lapide's comments show that the topic of Jesus' resurrection is taken more seriously by Christian and non-Christian scholars than many of us might think. Academic volumes are dedicated to the historical analysis of this incredible claim.[3]

But how we assess the plausibility of the resurrection depends not only on evidence but on our assumptions about the universe. If I assume that the observable laws of nature are the only things regulating the universe–that there is no Law-giver behind the laws–then claims of miracles such as the resurrection, no matter how widespread the historical evidence, will never seem rational to me. I will always opt for natural explanation. If, however, I hold that the laws of nature are not the only things regulating the universe–believing that there is a Law-giver behind these laws–then openness to a miraculous event like the resurrection can be considered rational so long as the evidence for the event is good.

By "evidence" for the resurrection, I do not mean of the repeatable, scientific kind. One of the things that has to be said loudly and often today is that science has a limited sphere of relevance on the question of truth. Scientists trade in the repeatable and/or observable. And within this sphere the scientific method works brilliantly. However, we must not demand an empirical form of evidence for events that are, by definition, unrepeatable. Otherwise you will rule out virtually all historical events (which, by definition, are unrepeatable and unobservable). The same logic would also rule out most legal judgements because, unless forensic analysis is involved, courts of law operate without recourse to science; instead, they weigh testimony, scrutinize motives, assess circumstances, and so on, just like the historian does.

The evidence for the resurrection of Jesus is good in the sense that we have the kind of historical evidence you would expect to be left behind if a man did in fact rise again, and more evidence pointing in that direction than you would expect if he did not. Put another way, there is a resurrection-shaped "dent" in the historical record. This is why the topic is still taken seriously, even by those who do not personally believe that a resurrection is possible.

THE TWO "FACTS" OF THE RESURRECTION STORY

Two facts form the resurrection-shaped dent: an empty tomb and eyewitness testimony. Let me explore these briefly before unpacking what the resurrection, if true, means for the Christian faith.

Most scholars agree that the tomb in which Jesus was laid was *empty* shortly after his burial. This judgement is based on a few things. First, there are at least three independent references to the empty tomb (by Mark, John and Paul, in texts that most scholars agree were composed without knowledge of the other). The criterion of multiple attestation says that when independent sources offer roughly the same portrait of an event from the past, that event takes on greater plausibility. Second, without supposing an empty tomb there appears to be no other way of explaining how Jesus' resurrection could have been proclaimed *in Jerusalem* (the site of Jesus' burial) without the tomb being checked and a body being produced as counter-evidence. The empty tomb could easily have been announced outside of Jerusalem (in Rome or Corinth, for example) where there was little risk of disconfirmation. But we know beyond a doubt that the resurrection was first announced in the city of Jesus' death and burial. This strongly suggests that the empty tomb was a given.

Confirmation of this, third, is found in the Jewish counter-claim to the resurrection. We know that from very early on the Jewish leadership claimed the disciples had stolen the body of Jesus from the tomb.[4] This is significant: it reveals that the first critics of the Christian movement in Jerusalem conceded that the tomb was empty (why else offer such a counter-claim!). They just disputed how it got that way.

Geza Vermes, the great Jewish scholar from Oxford University, regards it as "reasonably convincing" that "the entourage of Jesus discovered an empty tomb and were definite that it was the tomb." He also notes in passing that "the rumour that the apostles stole that body is most improbable."[5]

The empty tomb provides the essential circumstantial evidence for the claim of the witnesses that Jesus rose again. It does not prove the claim, of course, but it is the one circumstance that has to be in place for the claim to be taken at all seriously – by both folk in the first century and by scholars and people today.

But, of course, an empty tomb by itself can be interpreted in a number of ways. In the end, it is its combination with a second fact that moves scholars to treat the resurrection seriously: the testimony of eyewitnesses claiming to have seen him alive again.

It is a fact beyond dispute that significant numbers of men and women claimed to be eyewitnesses to the risen Jesus.

There are plenty of places we could turn: just about every one of the twenty-seven books of the New Testament attests to the experience of the witnesses. In fact, the point is not even in dispute in contemporary scholarship. That people claimed to have seen Jesus alive is a fact of history. As noted earlier, even as sceptical a scholar as Ed Sanders includes this in his list of undisputed facts about Jesus:

> There are no substantial doubts about the general course of Jesus' life: when and where he lived, approximately when and where he died, and the sort of thing that he did during his public activity.... We may add here a short list of equally secure facts about the aftermath of Jesus' life: his disciples fled; they saw him (in what sense is not certain) after his death; as a consequence, they believed that he would return to found the kingdom; they formed a community to await his return and sought to win others to faith in him as God's Messiah.[6]

The most significant text about the witnesses to the resurrection is found in the first New Testament letter of Paul to the Corinthians, the passage containing the early creed discussed in chapter 16:

> For what I received I passed on to you as of first importance: that Christ died for our sins according to the Scriptures, that he was buried, that he was raised on the third day according to the Scriptures, and that he appeared to Cephas, and then to the Twelve. After that, he appeared to more than five hundred of the brothers and sisters at the same time, most of whom are still living, though some have fallen asleep. Then he appeared to James, then to all the apostles, and last of all appeared to me also, as to one abnormally born (1 Corinthians 15:3–8).

We need to be clear about what this statement is. It is the testimony of someone who not only personally knew the witnesses listed here but who also claimed to have seen Jesus for himself. It is firsthand, eyewitness testimony.

Moreover, the statements found in verses 3–5 (from "that Christ died" to "then to the Twelve") can be dated very close in time to Jesus: "within months of Jesus' death," says James Dunn, no Christian apologist.[7] Even scholars who remain utterly sceptical about the resurrection itself agree that these statements about witnesses to the resurrection come from the period immediately after Jesus.[8] The upshot of this is that, whatever else the story of Christ's resurrection is, it cannot be the result of a growing legend. The early date of these reports just will not allow that interpretation.

The next most significant passages about the resurrection for the contemporary historian are probably the ones that list *women* as the first witnesses of the empty tomb and the risen Jesus. The four Gospels all agree that the first people to know about these things were not the male apostles at all, but the devoted female disciples:

> Now, very early on Sunday morning, the women who had come with Jesus from Galilee found the stone door rolled away from the tomb, but when they went in they did not find the body of the Lord Jesus. And as they stood there perplexed about this, suddenly two men in gleaming clothes approached them. The men said to them, "Why do you search for the living among the dead? He is not here; he has been raised!" The women returned from the tomb and told all these things to the eleven apostles and all the other people there. The women were Mary Magdalene, Joanna, Mary the mother of James, and some others with them (Luke 24:1–10).[9]

For historians, this is very interesting. As I mentioned briefly in chapter 14, women's testimony was widely regarded in the first century as invalid. Josephus captures the attitude of the time: "From women let no evidence be accepted, because of the levity and temerity of their sex."[10] Similarly, an ancient legal ruling from Palestine reads, "The law governing an oath of testimony applies to men and not to women, to those who are suitable to bear witness and not to those who are unsuitable to bear witness."[11] Given the low status of female testimony in the ancient world, why did all of the Gospel writers include women as the original witnesses of these strange events? This is a puzzle.

In historical analysis a key test for historical worth is what's called the criterion of embarrassment. This affirms that reports that are likely to have caused some embarrassment to a writer, but are nonetheless offered, are likely to be reliable (since we tend not to make ourselves look silly in public if we can help it). Lawyers call this "evidence against interest" and it is an important principle of legal scrutiny today. Based on this logic, most scholars writing about this topic believe it is very, very unlikely that the early Christians would have invented a story about women being the founding witnesses to the empty tomb and resurrection. It just would not have enhanced the credibility of their claim; quite the opposite. The most plausible conclusion is that a group of Jesus' women followers really did discover an empty tomb and really were the first to announce his resurrection.

There is little doubt, in other words, that from the very beginning numbers of men and women claimed to be eyewitnesses to the risen Jesus. But how do we know this testimony was sincere? Couldn't the first disciples have colluded, stolen the body and propounded a far-reaching fraud? The answer is: yes, of course, it is possible. I know of no serious scholar, however, who thinks this at all likely. First, those who supposedly invented this large-scale deception at the same time preserved sayings of their master calling for absolute honesty:

> I tell you, do not swear an oath at all: either by heaven,
> for it is God's throne; or by the earth, for it is his footstool;
> or by Jerusalem, for it is the city of the Great King. And
> do not swear by your head, for you cannot make even one
> hair white or black. All you need to say is simply "Yes," or
> "No"; anything beyond this comes from the evil one (Matthew 5:34–37).

Independently, the same saying is preserved by James the brother of Jesus, another claimed eyewitness (and therefore co-conspirator in the supposed fraud): "Above all, my brothers and sisters, do not swear—not by heaven or by earth or by anything else. All you need to say is a simple 'Yes' or 'No.' Otherwise you will be condemned" (James 5:12). One could perhaps argue that this call for absolute truth-telling was part of the cover needed to inspire credibility, but this would involve a rather arbitrary kind of scepticism.

The second reason scholars accept that the original testimony was utterly sincere is that there appears to be no adequate motive for deception. If the witnesses had benefited from their testimony – gained wealth, comfort or social status – we might well apply Cicero's famous legal dictum *cui bono,* "who benefits?" Witnesses with something to gain through their testimony should rarely be taken on face value. But the first followers of Jesus were in the opposite category. They experienced social estrangement, loss of property, loss of religious status (certainly in the case of Paul), imprisonment, whippings and even death. We have clear evidence of the execution of at least four of the key eyewitnesses to the risen Jesus: John Zebedee, James the brother of Jesus, Peter and Paul.[12] It is true that fanatics sometimes die for causes they merely *believe* to be true, but these first Christian martyrs were in a position to know whether or not the "cause" was a fabrication. And yet they willingly gave their lives for their testimony to the risen Jesus. Reflection on this point leads Ed Sanders to concede: "I do not regard deliberate fraud as a worthwhile explanation. Many of the people in these lists (of witnesses) were to spend the rest of their lives proclaiming that they had seen the risen Lord, and several of them would die for their cause."[13] For slightly different reasons, Jewish scholar Geza Vermes is equally dismissive of the suggestion that the disciples "faked" a resurrection:

> The rumour that the apostles stole that body is most improbable. From the psychological point of view, they would have been too depressed and shaken to be capable of such a dangerous undertaking. But above all, since neither they nor anyone else expected a resurrection, there would have been no purpose in faking one.[14]

There is no hard proof for the resurrection of Jesus. But we do have just the sort of evidence a resurrection would leave behind: an empty tomb and numerous eyewitnesses, several of whom died for the claim. This is why historians take the resurrection story more seriously than many of us realise. They agree that something very strange happened – that there is a resurrection-shaped dent in the historical record.

EXPLAINING (AWAY) THE HISTORY

This is where historical analysis leads us. It is also where it leaves us. How we go on from here to explain the data involves our prior assumptions. Most professional scholars do not attempt to explain away the empty tomb and the eyewitnesses. They tend to remain agnostic about what explains these data. I have already quoted Ed Sanders' simple confession, "What the reality was that gave rise to the (resurrection) experiences I do not know." A similar statement was made recently by Prof James Charlesworth of Princeton Theological Seminary, director of the Princeton Dead Sea Scrolls Project and a leading authority on ancient Judaism and Christianity. He speaks for many when he writes:

> The historian also observes evidence that unexpectedly a blazing zeal launches a massive missionary mission within Second Temple Judaism. It is headed by Peter and then Paul. Each of them is credited with a resurrection experience. Most historians imagine that without something happening, the Palestinian Jesus Movement would have drowned in lost hopes.[15]

What that "something" was cannot be determined by historical analysis alone. It involves our other beliefs. As I pointed out earlier, if I assume that the laws of nature are the only things regulating the universe, I will opt for a naturalistic explanation; any explanation, even a highly implausible one, is better than accepting an unnatural event such as a resurrection. However, if I accept the existence of a Law-giver behind the laws of nature, I can look at the evidence and feel rationally justified in accepting the claim that Jesus was raised from the dead. Indeed, I personally would go further and say that the resurrection is exactly the sort of event you would expect to happen if God really did exist, for it would offer us unique but tangible evidence of his presence in history. The life, death and (especially) the resurrection of Jesus is the X marking the spot most of humanity has been looking for: a concrete sign of the Creator's interest in our affairs.

CHAPTER 18

WHAT JESUS EXPECTED

A STORY IS TOLD ABOUT A YOUNG DESERTER IN THE ARMY OF ALEX-ander the Great (I have not been able to verify the story, but it ought to be true!). As Alexander moved eastward–through Persia toward India–conditions became tough and soldiers began to desert. Typically, such cowards were shown no mercy. They would be hunted down by Alexander's loyal guard and killed. But in this case the man who had secretly left the camp in search of

Mosaic floor
at the earliest
Christian prayer
hall in Megiddo

freedom and comfort was dealt a better fate. After being found and brought back, he stood guilty in the presence of the most powerful man on earth. For reasons unknown Alexander apparently decided to let the man go unpunished, but not before asking his name. "My name is Alexander, my King, just like yours," said the deserter. The battle-weary monarch replied in words that I can only imagine left an impression: "Young man, change your life or change your name!"

In just about every way, Alexander and Jesus were very different leaders. The one conquered nations with unprecedented might, the other with sacrificial love. But there is a truth in Alexander's words that every follower of Christ recognises. To call oneself a "Christian" is to hold the name of the greater King, Christ. And it will change your life.

The challenge of Jesus' resurrection is not just an historical one. It is one that invites us to examine our convictions about the world and our preferences for life. The first Christians said the risen Jesus sent them into the world not as journalists with an unusual news event to report but as ambassadors calling on people to acknowledge the divinely appointed King. It was a mission that utterly transformed the world:

> While the disciples were talking about the news of Jesus' resurrection, Jesus stood right in the middle of them and said, "Peace to you." But they were startled and terrified, because they thought they were seeing a ghost. And Jesus said to them, "Why are you disturbed, and why do doubts arise in your hearts? Look at my hands and feet, for it is really me. Touch me and see, for a ghost does not have flesh and bones, as you can see I have." Then he opened their minds to understand the Scriptures and said, "This is what is written: the Christ will suffer and rise from the dead on the third day, and repentance for the forgiveness of sins will be announced in his name to all nations, beginning from Jerusalem. You are witnesses of these things" (Luke 24:36–47).

FORGIVENESS FOR ALL

In different ways all the sources say the same thing. Jesus sent his disciples out with the message about God's mercy, or what Luke's

Gospel just quoted describes as "repentance for the forgiveness of sins." The challenge was personal. It was the logical extension of Jesus' own career. He had preached judgement and yet constantly invited people to his table of friendship and forgiveness. The disciples now took this message to Jerusalem, to Israel, and to the whole world.

Megiddo is the site of the earliest church building yet found. This strategic trade city contains the remains of a Christian prayer hall dating to the early third century with three mosaic inscriptions pointing to its Christian use, one of which indicates that this community was probably made up of Greeks and Romans, not Jews. The words commemorate a Roman army officer who contributed to the mosaic's construction. It is early physical evidence of the extraordinary reach of the Christian message. What started as an exclusively Jewish movement soon became an international movement.

But the message was the same.

Another of the inscriptions in this prayer hall hails the "God Jesus Christ," putting the lie to the oft-made claim, at least in popular works like Dan Brown's *The Da Vinci Code*, that it was Emperor Constantine in the fourth century who invented the idea of Jesus' divinity. That idea, too, belongs to the first generation of witnesses to Jesus, as has been shown by Prof Larry Hurtado of the University of Edinburgh in his *How on Earth Did Jesus Become a God?*[1] Also appearing on the mosaic floor is the early Christian symbol of a fish. The Greek word for "fish," *ichthus*, is an anagram of the Greek words *Iesous Christos Theou Yios Soter*: "Jesus Christ, God's Son, Saviour." Contained in this symbol, then, is the two-fold message of historic Christianity: the status of Jesus as the Christ or Son of God and his mission as the Saviour, the one who died for the forgiveness of the world. This ancient prayer hall is a kind of monument to the seriousness with which the first followers of Jesus took his words, "repentance for the forgiveness of sins will be announced in my name to all nations, beginning from Jerusalem." Men and women from all walks of life have throughout the centuries and today found the forgiveness of sins Jesus promised. It is at the very heart of real Christianity.

Some years ago, I was in video trouble. I had simply forgotten to return a film; in fact, it had fallen behind the television, out of sight and out of mind. No letter arrived from the video store, and months went past before we looked behind the TV and the video tumbled into view. It turned out that the video was six months overdue and the "extended viewing fees" must have amounted to a couple of hundred dollars. To return or not to return, that is the question. To face the music and pay the fine, or to act as if nothing were wrong and no fine was mounting, that was the ethical dilemma.

Just at this very tricky point, a postcard arrived in the mailbox from the video store, addressed personally. It was not demanding payment or chastising the recipient for his misdemeanours (both of which would have been completely within reason). No, the card announced something entirely unexpected: WE'RE WIPING THE SLATE CLEAN. I turned it over and read the words: "We would like to welcome you back to our store and 'wipe the slate clean.' Simply bring in this postcard to your local video store and we will remove all extended viewing fees, no questions asked."

In disbelief, I grabbed the video, rushed to the store, postcard in hand. I eagerly, and somewhat sheepishly, showed the card to the store attendant. Although the smirk on her face was not entirely non-judgemental, she did do what the card promised. She called up the "Dickson, J" file on the computer, went to the "fees and fines" column and inserted a beautiful zero.

It was only as I left the store that I realised that what had just happened was a perfect gift to someone who spends his time trying to explain what Christianity is all about. God is in the business of "wiping the slate clean." God knows that the debt we owe him—all of our wrong-doing, our failures to live a life of love, all of our sin—is profound and unpayable. But God is willing to wipe the slate clean, to forgive and forget. The attitude of the video store to a wayward customer is a tiny—though I hope not trivializing—insight into the profound mercy and graciousness of God captured in Jesus' promise of "forgiveness of sins to all nations."

"REPENTANCE" EXPLAINED

But God's mercy is not automatic simply because the Messiah has died and risen to life. It came only to those who experienced what Jesus called "repentance." The message he gave to the first heralds was "repentance for the forgiveness of sins."

Repentance has bad connotations today. For many it conjures up images of the old-fashioned, pulpit-thumping, fire-and-brimstone preacher. For the truth we have to look a little further back in time. The word "repent" is a very ancient Jewish term. Jesus was raised on the writings of the Old Testament prophets. Many of them pleaded with Israel to take God more seriously, and the word they used was "repent." John the Baptist also preached "a baptism of repentance." Likewise, Jesus, when challenged by the religious elite for wining and dining with the irreligious, responded: "I have not come to call the righteous, but sinners to repentance."

In the Gospels the word "repentance" is the Greek term *metanoia*. It literally means "change-of-mind." This takes us to the heart of what Jesus expected of his hearers, and of what his disciples echoed throughout the Roman world. People were to change their minds – about God, themselves and, of course, about Jesus. Concerning God they were to acknowledge his absolute authority over all things. Concerning themselves they were to admit they deserved divine judgement for their failure to love God and neighbour. And concerning Jesus they were to accept not only his status as the Christ but also the forgiveness for which he died as the Saviour. The change-of-mind was comprehensive.

The point is worth stressing because so often in the history of Christianity Jesus' demand for *metanoia*, change-of-mind, has been heard as a call simply to improve behaviour – to pull your socks up, to be nice, honest, pure and so on. But the word is not *metamorphosis*, the change-of-*form* or conduct, but *metanoia*, the deeper change of our hearts and minds. Naturally, those who "change their mind" about God, themselves and Jesus will *change*. The life of Jesus has always transformed the lives of his followers. But changing behaviour was not the core of Jesus' message – despite the fact that this has sometimes been the obsession of the church.

There is no question the Jesus of history wanted more from his hearers than improved morality. He wanted a revolution deep inside the minds and hearts of every man and woman. On the one hand, this involved turning away from our own path – our own cultural norms and traditions – and accepting the path that Jesus taught, the path of love for God and neighbour.

But perhaps the most important part of what Jesus called repentance was trusting him for God's forgiveness, the forgiveness for which he said he died. Just as the sinners of his day recognised him as their only hope of divine mercy, and just as the prodigal son looked to the awaiting father for undeserved pardon, so when we repent we are really turning from trusting our own morality to trusting his mercy. It is in this way that the life of the historical Jesus has continued to challenge and inspire the lives of countless millions ever since.

THERE ARE PLENTY OF BARRIERS TO PEOPLE TODAY ACCEPTING Jesus' message of repentance for the forgiveness of sins. Secular society tells us we would be better off without religion, and some people accept that without examining whether it is true. In fact, on balance the Christian religion has brought more good than harm to the world, even acknowledging that it has sometimes messed up very badly.

There have been a lot of studies in recent times about the positive contribution Christianity has made, in particular, to the West. Sociologist Rodney Stark has written a series of books in which he provides evidence and arguments for the view that if we had not had Christianity, we might not have developed good things such as human equality regardless of race or sex, freedom from slavery, economic growth, human rights and social welfare. All of these social goods can be connected to the outworking of Christian teachings, claims Stark. Christianity also contributed to the rise of capitalism, the establishment of democracy and even

Temple Mount steps west of the Dome of the Spirits—the bottom step may have been the northwest corner of Solomon's temple wall enclosure

Copyright 1995–2010 Phoenix Data Systems

the development of science (as has recently been shown by Peter Harrison, professor of Science and Religion at the University of Oxford).[1] These are, of course, major claims that need to be explored in detail, but there is general agreement among historians, economists and sociologists that many of the values that the West holds dear are associated with the growth of Christianity throughout the middle ages. Even avowedly "secular" political philosophers, such as Prof Jürgen Habermas of the Johann Wolfgang Goethe University in Frankfurt, openly concede the influence of Christianity on Western social thought:

> Christianity has functioned for the normative self-understanding of modernity as more than a mere precursor or a catalyst. Egalitarian universalism, from which sprang the ideas of freedom and social solidarity, of an autonomous conduct of life and emancipation, of the individual morality of conscience, human rights and democracy, is the direct heir to the Judaic ethic of justice and the Christian ethic of love. This legacy, substantially unchanged, has been the object of continual critical appropriation and reinterpretation. To this day, there is no alternative to it. And in light of the current challenges of a postnational constellation [he means, I think, the European Union and the like], we continue to draw on the substance of this heritage. Everything else is just idle postmodern talk.[2]

There is therefore a huge disconnect between the popular claim that the church is responsible for most personal and social evils, and the evidence that it has actually brought a great deal of good to society. If people feel negatively toward the church, it may be worth reading about some of the good it has done, if only to be a little more balanced.

OVERCOMING BARRIERS

Some of us just feel angry with the church, and that stops us from going any further in our faith journey. Whether it's for starting wars, or for abusing children in church schools, or just a grudge against a priest you didn't like, people get put off by Jesus because they were put off the by church. I think we need to separate out those two things.

Terrible things have indeed been done by Christians, even by those in positions of trust and authority. It is not surprising that those who have been wronged feel incredibly antagonistic to the religious views of those who wronged them. In our time, one of the most heinous discoveries has been the level of sexual abuse of children that has taken place within churches or church-run institutions. This is shameful and dreadful, and it is a very good thing that people are being brought to justice and punished for their crimes against vulnerable children who were placed in their care. There is no excuse for such behaviour, and it brings terrible disrepute to the Christian faith itself.

I can only plead with people to recognise that such behaviour is itself anti-Christian and should not happen; it is sinful and wrong and repulsive. It may take a very long time for someone who has suffered like this to give even the real Jesus the time of day. But I sincerely hope that it is possible, because Jesus outshines his flawed followers in every possible way.

Others find it difficult to take Christianity seriously because they cannot stand what they see as Christianity's moral restrictions. Drinking, smoking, sex, fashion sense. Christianity seems way behind the times in these areas. In an age where it is incredibly common to have sex outside of marriage, to have many partners, to accept variations on the male-female partnership, and to view pornography, the Christian faith can just seem antiquated and irrelevant.

Actually, people often accept a caricature of Christian teachings on this. Christians are not anti-sex – I do not know how that idea hangs around. Christians do have particular views about sex and sexuality, but sex is viewed positively in the Bible and it is a shame that this is not well known. In fact, the Bible teaches that sex is for pleasure, that partners ought to seek to please each other, and that, enjoyed in its proper context, sex is important for a good partnership.

Likewise, Christians can drink and smoke – together if they like! You will not find any anti-drinking teaching in the Bible. You will find instructions to avoid drunkenness, but again the Christian teaching is that alcohol is part of the Good Life, as long as it is "enjoyed responsibly," as the wine labels say. Smoking might be dumb for health reasons, but it is not forbidden in Scripture.

I won't even try to defend Christians against the fashion complaint, except to suggest that perhaps those people dressed badly before they were Christians! But, seriously, I would hope people can look at the whole package of Christian living, not just pull out superficial bits they don't like.

What I hope people will do is come to terms with their own hearts, and see their need for God. At the same time, I hope they can see that taking Christianity seriously is also a matter of engaging your mind in thinking, reading, debating and assessing history, ethics and ideas. It is about not getting too comfortable and complacent in your unbelief.

And then I hope people will give Jesus a chance, and examine who he really is. He addresses the heart, the mind–the hurting parts of us, as well as the rationally demanding parts. Christianity needs to be given a chance to put its best case forward, and that case is Jesus.

LITTLE STEPS IN THE RIGHT DIRECTION

I have a friend who works in my building and who has sniffed around Christianity for a very long time. He has attended introductory courses on the faith, listened to some half-decent sermons and even sat down for some serious chats. He is a deep searcher, a constant searcher.

We had coffee together recently and he laid out quibble after quibble, doubt after doubt, question after question. He has one of those personalities that has to cross every "t" and dot every "i" before making any move at all. He is a statistician so perhaps it comes from that detailed analytical mind. But I put it to him, "Can you imagine taking this approach with a relationship–needing to have all the information about someone before you offered anything of yourself to them?" His eyes said it all. "Oh, yes, I've done that once or twice," he admitted. "It's not entirely healthy!" No, it isn't. Relationships develop bit by bit. You give a little of yourself and you get a little back, until a friendship forms and deepens.

I tried to point out to my friend that Christian faith is much more like a relationship than a statistical analysis. Waiting to have every question answered before you make any move toward God is unhelpful and unrealistic. It is much better to take little steps toward the Maker in accordance with the measure of interest and faith you already have. If you believe there is some kind of Creator, speak to him, ask him to make himself clear. If you believe Jesus taught the truth about God, study his words and try to put them into practice. If you have a hunch that you need the mercy for which Christ died, call on him for forgiveness.

Take whatever size steps are appropriate to your situation. Little moves in the right direction are better than forever imagining taking one large leap of faith only *after* you've had every question answered.

INTRODUCTION

WELCOME TO THE *LIFE OF JESUS* VIDEO SMALL-GROUP EXPERIENCE. Over six sessions you will watch a full-scale video documentary, read the relevant chapters in this book, read one of the ancient biographies of Jesus (the Gospel of Luke) and discuss questions about one of history's most intriguing figures.

The purpose of this group study is straightforward: to provide the inquiring, the sceptical and believers alike with an opportunity to explore Jesus' life and to consider its significance for today. Whatever your current perspective, we are confident you will be informed and entertained.

The atmosphere ought to be open, questioning and practical, even if at times the material is challenging. Jesus was not a conformist, so it shouldn't surprise us if parts of his story contradict some of our current views of the world and of ourselves. If your group has a leader or facilitator, as we expect most will, it is his or her task to strike a balance between careful attention to the historical record and open-minded reflection on the relevance of Jesus' life today. A few helps for group leaders can be found at the end of the discussion guide (see page 197).

The Jesus presented in the course is not a "denominational" figure; he is not even particularly religious. He is the Jesus of history. We worked hard to provide viewers and readers with a portrait of the man from Galilee that is faithful to both the Gospel of Luke and contemporary scholarship on him.

In addition to reading the book and watching the video episode, you are invited to read the Gospel according to Luke. Unlike most modern biographies, Luke is very brief. In just twenty pages we move from the traditional Christmas stories in quiet Bethlehem to, the tragic events three decades later in the bustling city of Jerusalem. Luke's compact, punchy style takes a few pages to get used to but, once the rhythm is found, it sweeps us along to the story's dramatic climax. The English translation printed throughout this book and in the studies that follow is from *The Essential Jesus*. (Participants who want to obtain a copy of *The Essential Jesus*, published by Matthias Media, Sydney, Australia, can contact www.matthiasmedia.com.) But any modern translation, such as the *New International Version* or the *New Revised Standard Version*, will do the job well.

Jesus' life has had an enormous impact on the culture, morality and politics of the Western world and on the personal experience of countless millions of individuals throughout history. With this in mind, it is only natural to want to move beyond history and philosophy to consider the ongoing relevance of Jesus' claims today. The conversation-starter questions in each session are designed to facilitate further conversation about the practical relevance of Jesus' life and teaching. They are the heart of this group study. Whether you approach them as a springboard for group conversation or as a prompt for the facilitator's input, we are confident you will find these a rewarding part of the *Life of Jesus* experience.

The format of the six sessions is simple:

1. Prior to the session please read the related chapters of this book. If you don't have time, be sure to read them sometime before the next session.

2. Watch the corresponding *Life of Jesus* video episode (each no more than 20 minutes in length). Time permitting, feel free to have a brief question time clarifying anything said in this part of the documentary and the related book chapters.

3. Work your way through the three or four "Group Discussion Questions," allowing time for both random questions from participants and personal reflections from the facilitator. Critical opinions are always welcome. (30–40 minutes)

4. Read and consider the brief "Session Challenge" as a way to wrap up your time together. This is a simple statement

urging participants to consider the contemporary relevance of the material just studied and pointing to the relevant readings from Luke in preparation for the next study. (5 minutes)

I hope you enjoy exploring the fascinating figure at the heart of the Christian faith.

SESSION 1: GOD'S SIGNPOST

Jesus as a Tangible Sign of God's Interest in Our World

BEFORE THIS SESSION
If possible please read chapters 1–4 of this book.

VIDEO EPISODE
Please watch episode 1 of the *Life of Jesus* video. If you'd like to take some notes, use the space below.

GROUP DISCUSSION QUESTIONS

1. What have you learnt from this episode about the way historians approach the study of the life of Jesus? How did it (or did it not) surprise you?

2. At the centre of Jesus' worldview was the conviction that the Creator's existence and power are obvious to all. The Jewish Scriptures (or what Christians call the Old Testament) put it like this: "The heavens declare the glory of God; the skies proclaim the work of his hands" (Psalm 19:1). Why do you think this conviction about a Creator has been shared by most people throughout most of history?

Even today, the vast majority of people believe in some kind of "God." What practical relevance do you think this belief holds for the majority?

3. Please read Luke 1:1–4 below:

   [1] Many have attempted to put together an account of the things that have been fulfilled among us, [2] just as these things were passed on to us by those who from the beginning were eyewitnesses and servants of the message. [3] For this reason, it seemed good to me as well, having investigated everything thoroughly from the start, to write something orderly for you, Most Honourable Theophilus. [4] My aim is that you may know the certainty of the message you were taught.

   What elements of Luke's introduction to his Gospel suggest his intention to report truthfully about real historical events?

4. Please read the following passage from the documentary/book:

   At the heart of the world's largest faith (Christianity) is not a lone spiritual insight, a mystical story from the dawn of time or a dictation of divine words in a holy book, but a series of events that are said to have taken place in public, in datable time, recorded by a variety of witnesses. For better or worse, Christian Scripture is fundamentally different from other holy books. In the events of Jesus' life, death and resurrection believers claim to observe a tangible, testable sign directing us to the "kingdom of God."

   Is this claim arrogant or justified? Why or why not?

SESSION CHALLENGE

The claim of Christianity is that God has revealed himself in a tangible way in the history of Jesus as faithfully recorded in the Gospel of Luke (and the other New Testament Gospels). The life of Jesus is a "signpost" to God. As we read Luke, please contemplate not just the historical life of Jesus but also the spiritual life he offers us.

Before the next session please read Luke chapters 1–4.

SESSION 2: CHRISTOS

The Identity of Jesus and His Critique of "Religion"

BEFORE THE SESSION
If possible please read chapters 5–7 of this book.

VIDEO EPISODE
Please watch episode 2 of the *Life of Jesus* video. If you'd like to take some notes, use the space below.

GROUP DISCUSSION QUESTIONS

1. How do you tend to picture Jesus? In what ways has this video episode challenged your views?

2. Many people today hold favourable views about Jesus. What are some of the most popular today, and how do they compare with the claims of the Gospel of Luke?

3. Please read Luke 2:6–12 below:

⁶ And while they were there in Bethlehem, the time came for her to have the baby,⁷ and she gave birth to her firstborn son. And because there was no room for them in the inn, she used strips of cloth to wrap him up, and an animal food trough for his cradle. ⁸ In that part of the country, there were shepherds who stayed out in the fields at night to keep guard over their flock. ⁹ Without warning, one of the Lord's angels appeared to them, and the blinding brilliance of the Lord shone all around them. They were terrified, ¹⁰ but the angel said to them, "Do not be afraid. Listen, I am here to bring you news of great joy, which is for all the people: ¹¹ today, a Saviour has been born to you in the city of David. He is Christ the Lord. ¹² And this will be the sign for you—you will find a child wrapped up in strips of cloth and lying in a food trough (manger)."

How does this passage fulfill and/or challenge expectations about the role and majesty of the Jewish Messiah/Christ?

What does the manger (animal feeding trough) suggest about the future direction of Jesus' career?

4. In the middle of his adult career Jesus asked his disciples who they thought he was. Please read Luke 9:18–26 below where we find both the disciples' answer to the question and Jesus' challenging response. Then reflect on the following questions:

¹⁸ Once, while he was praying alone, with his disciples close by, he asked them a question: "Who do the crowds say that I am?" ¹⁹ And they answered, "John the Baptist; others say Elijah, and others that an ancient prophet has risen up." ²⁰ He said to them, "And you, who do you say I am?" Peter answered, "The Christ of God." ²¹ And he sternly commanded them not to say this to anyone, ²² saying, "The Son of Man must suffer many things, and be rejected by the elders and Chief Priests and scribes, and be killed, and on the third day be raised up."
²³ He said to them all, "If anyone wants to come after me, let him deny himself and pick up his cross each day, and follow me. ²⁴ For whoever wants to save his life will lose it; but whoever loses his life for my sake–he will save it. ²⁵ For what profit does a person get if he gains the whole world, but loses or forfeits his very self? ²⁶ For whoever is ashamed of me

and my words, the Son of Man will be ashamed of him when he comes in his glory and in the glory of the Father and the holy angels."

Despite the theme of humility that runs through the life of Jesus, what kind of authority does Jesus claim for himself in this passage?

At this moment, how would you answer the question Jesus put to his disciples ("Who do you say I am?")? What factors have influenced your view?

SESSION CHALLENGE

Whatever our personal impressions of Jesus, the claim we are urged to consider is that he is the Christ, the one who speaks and acts for God. He calls on all of us to "follow" him.

Before the next session please read Luke chapters 5–11.

Jesus' Vision of the Future and Its Relevance Now

BEFORE THE SESSION

If possible please read chapters 8 – 10 of this book.

VIDEO EPISODE

Please watch episode 3 of the *Life of Jesus* video. If you'd like to take some notes, use the space below.

GROUP DISCUSSION QUESTIONS

1. Prior to watching this video episode, what would you have said was the heart of Jesus' message? How, if at all, has this episode caused you to rethink your perspective?

2. Please read the following two passages from Luke pondering what Jesus is saying about the kingdom of God:

LUKE 6:20 – 31

20 Then he turned his attention to his disciples, and said, "Blessed are you who are poor, because the kingdom of God belongs to you.
21 Blessed are you who are hungry now, because you will be fed. Blessed are you who weep now, because you will laugh. 22 Blessed are you when people hate you and reject you and criticise you and blacken your name on account of the Son of Man. 23 Rejoice and leap for joy in that day, for great is your reward in heaven; for the ancestors of those who persecute you used to do the same to the prophets.

24 "But, woe to you who are rich, because you are receiving your comfort. 25 Woe to you who are full now, because you will be hungry. Woe to you who laugh now, because you will mourn and weep. 26 Woe to you when everyone speaks well of you, for their ancestors used to do the same to the false prophets.

27 "But to you who are listening, I say: Love your enemies. Do good to those who hate you. 28 Bless those who curse you. Pray for those who mistreat you. 29 If someone strikes you on the cheek, offer him the other cheek as well; and if someone takes your coat, let him have your shirt as well. 30 To everyone who asks of you, give; and if someone takes your things, don't demand them back. 31 And in the way you want people to treat you, do the same for them."

LUKE 13:18 – 30

18 Jesus said, "What is the kingdom of God like and to what shall I compare it? 19 It is like a mustard seed that someone took and threw into his garden. It grew and became a tree, and the birds of the air nested in its branches." 20 Again he said, "To what shall I compare the kingdom of God? 21 It is like yeast that a woman took and mixed into a large amount of flour until the whole batch of dough was leavened."

22 Jesus was travelling through various cities and towns, teaching in them, as he continued his journey toward Jerusalem. 23 Someone asked him, "Lord, will only a small number of people be rescued?" And he replied to them, 24 "Strive to enter through the narrow door. For, I tell you, once the owner of the house gets up and locks the door, many will try to enter but not be able to. 25 You will stand outside and begin to knock on the door, saying, 'Lord, open up for us!' But he will say in reply, 'I do not know where you come from.' 26 Then you will begin to say, 'We ate and drank with you and you taught in our streets.' 27 But he will say to you, 'I do not know where you come from. Get away from me, all of you doers of injustice!' 28 In that place there will be weeping and grinding of teeth, when you see Abraham and Isaac and Jacob and all the prophets inside the kingdom of God, but you yourselves thrown out of it. 29 Yet, people from east and west, from north and south, will come and recline at the dining table in the kingdom of God. 30 Indeed, some who are now last will be first, and some who are now first will be last."

What do you find attractive in Jesus' teaching about God's kingdom? Why?

What elements of Jesus' teaching about the kingdom do you find less appealing? Why?

3. Please read the following passage from the video concerning the meaning of Jesus' healings:

> For Jesus, his healings were not sorcery, trickery or even proofs of power. They were signs that the kingdom of God had arrived. According to the Old Testament, God's kingdom would overthrow evil and restore health and harmony to the world. That's what Jesus thought was going on when he cast out evil spirits and restored sick bodies. As strange as it sounds today, Jesus was offering a preview of the kingdom, of the time when God will put everything right in this world.

How does the idea that Jesus' healings were intended as "signs" of the future kingdom differ from any ideas you might have had previously? (For more information on this concept skim chapter 9.)

If Jesus' promise about the kingdom of God is true, what comfort does it offer those who have ever wished God would "do something about the mess in the world"?

SESSION CHALLENGE

Jesus promised (in his teaching and healings) that God's kingdom would one day make everything right in the world. He asks us not only to hope for the future kingdom but to live now by its Golden Rule of love.

Before the next session please read Luke chapters 12–18.

SESSION 4: JUDGE AND FRIEND

Jesus' Thoughts on "Religious Hypocrites" and "Rotten Sinners"

BEFORE THE SESSION

If possible please read chapters 11–13 of this book.

VIDEO EPISODE

Please watch episode 4 of the *Life of Jesus* video. If you'd like to take some notes, use the space below.

GROUP DISCUSSION QUESTIONS

1. Have you ever tried to resolve the tension between the fact that Jesus teaches both divine judgement and divine mercy? How has this video episode helped you to resolve the paradox?

2. Please read Luke 10:8–16, 25–28 below, passages in which Jesus warns the general population of God's judgement and makes clear what is God's standard:

   ^{8} "When you go into a city and they welcome you, eat what they set before you. ^{9} Heal the sick there and tell them, "The kingdom of God is near–almost upon you." ^{10} But if you enter a city and they do not welcome you, go out into its streets and say, ^{11} 'We even wipe off the dust that clings to our feet from your city! But know this: the kingdom of God is near.' [12] I say to you that it will be more tolerable for Sodom on the day of judgement than for that city. [13] Woe to you, Chorazin; woe to you, Bethsaida! For if the powerful deeds that have happened in you had taken place in Tyre and Sidon long ago, they would have repented in sackcloth and ashes. [14] But it will be more tolerable for Tyre and Sidon in the judgement than for you. [15] And you, Capernaum, will you be lifted up to the heavens? No, you will go down to hell."

[25] Just then, a certain expert in the Jewish law stood up, wanting to test Jesus. "Teacher," he said, "What must I do so that I will inherit eternal life?" [26] And he said to him, "What is written in the Law? How do you read it?" [27] The lawyer replied, "Love the Lord your God with all your heart and with all your soul and with all your strength and with all your mind; and love your neighbour as yourself." [28] Jesus said to him, "You have answered correctly. Do this, and you will live." [29] But the lawyer wanted to justify himself; so he said to Jesus, "And who is my neighbour?"

Many today avoid thinking of Jesus as a preacher of judgement, preferring to emphasise his loving acceptance. Why do you think this is?

For Jesus, God's standard is two-fold: to love the Creator with all our heart, and our neighbours as ourselves. What do you think Jesus might say (a) to the modern religious person who prays and attends church but shows little compassion toward others?; (b) to the modern humanitarian who is compassionate toward others but neglects the Creator himself?

3. Please read Luke 15:1–3, 11–32, where Jesus tells the famous parable of the prodigal son (NOTE: the younger son in the story represents the "sinners" in Jesus' audience, the older son represents the "religious" leaders and the father represents God):

[1] Now all the tax collectors and sinners were gathering near to listen to Jesus. [2] But the Pharisees and the Scribes were grumbling and saying, "This man welcomes sinners and eats meals with them." [3] So he told them this parable ...

[11] "There was a man who had two sons. [12] The younger one said to his father, 'Father, give me my share of the inheritance.' The father then divided the property between the two sons. [13] Soon afterwards, the

younger son collected everything together and travelled to a distant land, where he squandered his inheritance on reckless living. [14] After he had spent everything, there was a great famine in that land, and he began to be in need. [15] So he went and hired himself out to a citizen of that land, who sent him out to his fields to feed pigs. [16] And he was longing to feed himself with the pods that the pigs were eating; yet no-one gave him anything. [17] Then he came to his senses and thought, 'How many of my father's employees have an abundance of food, and yet here I am dying of hunger. [18] I'll get up and go to my father and say to him, "I have sinned toward God and before you. [19] I am no longer worthy to be called your son. Make me like one of your employees."' [20] So he got up and went to his father.

"He was still some distance away when his father caught sight of him. The father was deeply moved, and running to his son he embraced him and kissed him. [21] The son said, 'Father, I have sinned toward God and before you. I am no longer worthy to be called your son.'

[22] "But the father said to his servants, 'Quick, bring out the best robe and dress him in it; put a ring on his finger and shoes on his feet. [23] Bring the fattened calf and kill it. Let's eat and celebrate, [24] because this son of mine was dead but now is alive again; he was lost but now is found.' And they began to celebrate.

[25] "Now the elder son had been in the field, and as he drew near the house he heard music and dancing. [26] And calling one of the hired hands, he asked what this was all about. [27] He replied, 'Your brother has come and your father has killed the fattened calf, because he has got him back safe and well.'

[28] "The elder son became furious and refused even to enter the house. But his father went outside and pleaded with him. [29] He answered his father, 'Look! I have been slaving for you for so many years, and I have never disobeyed your command. Yet you have never given me even a goat so that I could have a celebration with my friends. [30] But when this son of yours, who has squandered your estate on prostitutes, comes home, you kill the fattened calf for him!'

[31] "But his father said to him, 'My child, you are always with me, and everything that is mine is yours. [32] But we must celebrate and rejoice, because this brother of yours was dead but now is alive, and was lost but now is found.' "

Through this parable what is Jesus saying about (a) what makes someone a "sinner"; (b) what God is like; (c) what is wrong with religious self-righteousness?

Does Jesus' picture of God in this parable contradict his teaching about judgement? Why or why not?

SESSION CHALLENGE

The Jesus of the New Testament warned of God's judgement on all who failed to love God and neighbour. Yet, he also announced a lavish offer of forgiveness. He calls on us all to acknowledge our sin and return to the Creator for mercy.

Before the next session please read Luke chapters 19–23.

SESSION 5: CROSS EXAMINATION

BEFORE THE SESSION
If possible please read chapters 14–16 of this book.

VIDEO EPISODE
Please watch episode 5 of the *Life of Jesus* video. If you'd like to take some notes, use the space below.

GROUP DISCUSSION QUESTIONS

1. Does the idea of God requiring a blood sacrifice bother you? Has this video episode helped your understanding? Why or why not?

2. Please read Isaiah 53:3–11, an Old Testament prophecy written centuries before Christ that predicts a mysterious "servant" of God who would suffer for the sake of others (NOTE: the past tense was often used in prophecy to emphasise the certainty of fulfillment):

   [3] He was despised and rejected by others, a man of sorrows, and familiar with pain. Like one from whom people hide their faces he was despised, and we held him in low esteem. [4] Surely he took up our pain and bore our suffering, yet we considered him punished by God, stricken by him, and afflicted. [5] But he was pierced for our transgressions, he was crushed for

our iniquities; the punishment that brought us peace was on him, and by his wounds we are healed. [6] We all, like sheep, have gone astray, each of us has turned to his own way; and the LORD has laid on him the iniquity of us all. [7] He was oppressed and afflicted, yet he did not open his mouth; he was led like a lamb to the slaughter, and as a sheep before its shearers is silent, so he did not open his mouth ... [11] After he has suffered, he will see the light of life and be satisfied; by his knowledge my righteous servant will justify many, and he will bear their iniquities.

What similarities do you observe between this Old Testament passage and Jesus' words about his death at his Last Supper ("This is my body which is given for you.... This cup is the new covenant in my blood, which is poured out for you")?

How do you think Jesus might have answered the modern complaint that God ought to forgive people without any sacrifice?

3. Please read the following crucifixion account from Luke 23:32–46:

[32] Two others who were criminals were also led out with him to be executed. [33] And when they arrived at the place called "The Skull," they crucified him there along with the criminals – one on Jesus' right, the other on his left. [34] And the soldiers divided his clothing by placing bets; [35] and the people stood by, watching. The leaders even made fun of him, saying, "He rescued others, let him rescue himself if he really is God's Christ, his Chosen One." [36]The soldiers also ridiculed him, coming up and offering him bitter wine. [37] They said, "If you really are the King of the Jews, rescue yourself." [38] There was a placard above him which read: THIS IS THE KING OF THE JEWS. [39] One of the criminals who hung there was abusing Jesus, saying, "Aren't you supposed to be the Christ? Rescue yourself and us."

[40] But the other criminal responded with a rebuke: "Have you no fear of God? After all, you are under the same death sentence. [41] Yet, we are here justly; we are receiving what we deserve for our actions, but he has done nothing wrong." [42] Then he said, "Jesus, please remember me when you come into your kingdom." [43] And Jesus replied, "I tell you the truth, today you will be with me in Paradise."

[44] By this time, it was already about midday, but darkness came over the whole land until three in the afternoon, [45] because the sun stopped

shining. The curtain of the Temple was torn down the middle. [46] Then
Jesus cried out in a loud voice, "Father, into your hands I entrust my
spirit!" With these words he breathed his last breath.

Verses 40–43 are often described as a climax in Luke's Gospel, captur-
ing in a single paragraph key themes of Jesus' life. Why do you think
this is?

Thinking of this same paragraph and of the meaning of Jesus' death,
what do you think Luke (or Jesus) might say to the person who thinks
that moral behaviour and/or religious observance are the things that
atone for our sin before God?

SESSION CHALLENGE

The very crux of Christianity is the cross. Whatever the political realities
leading to his crucifixion, Jesus taught that it had spiritual significance.
He died so that God's judgement might pass over us onto him, so that
we might receive God's mercy. He calls us all–like the criminal on the
cross–to turn to him for forgiveness.

Before the next session please read Luke chapter 24.

How Could It Happen? What Does It Matter?

BEFORE THE SESSION

If possible please read chapters 17 – 19 of this book.

VIDEO EPISODE

Please watch episode 6 of the *Life of Jesus* video. If you'd like to take some notes, use the space below.

GROUP DISCUSSION QUESTIONS

1. What have you learnt from this video episode about the way historians view Jesus' resurrection story? Why is the challenge of the resurrection more than a simply historical question?

2. If it could be proved that Jesus did *not* rise from the dead, would it make a difference to the significance of Christianity? Why or why not?

3. Please read the final resurrection scene in Luke 24:36–47 below:

> 36 While they were talking about these things, Jesus stood right in the middle of them and said, "Peace to you." 37 But they were startled and terrified, because they thought they were seeing a ghost.
>
> 38 And Jesus said to them, "Why are you disturbed, and why do doubts arise in your hearts? 39 Look at my hands and feet, for it is really me. Touch me and see, for a ghost does not have flesh and bones, as

you can see I have." [40] He said this, and showed them his hands and feet. [41] But when they still did not believe because of joy and amazement, he said to them, "Do you have anything here I can eat?" [42] So they handed him a piece of cooked fish. [43] He took it and ate it right in front of them.

[44] Then he said to them, "I told you about these things while I was still with you: everything that is written about me in the Law of Moses, the Prophets and the Psalms had to be fulfilled." [45] Then he opened their minds to understand the Scriptures [46] and said, "This is what is written: the Christ will suffer and rise from the dead on the third day, [47] and repentance for the forgiveness of sins will be announced in his name to all nations, beginning from Jerusalem."

Jesus expected people to hear of his life, death and resurrection and experience "repentance" (*metanoia*), a profound change of mind. After all that you have read in the Gospel of Luke, what changes do you think Jesus expected in our attitude toward (a) God; (b) ourselves; (c) Jesus himself?

Some today find it very difficult to accept that "forgiveness of sins" is so freely available to all who repent. Why do you think this is?

4. What for you is the most significant thing about the life of Jesus?

SESSION CHALLENGE

Christianity proclaims not just a Jesus of history, but one who lives and reigns today. Jesus Christ urges each one of us to accept God's way (repentance) and so enjoy forgiveness of sins and a place in God's kingdom.

The Lord's Prayer, taught by Jesus, is an expression of trust in God, a plea for forgiveness and a request that God's kingdom would shape our lives here and now. Praying these words is one very appropriate response to the challenge of the life of Jesus.

Our Father in heaven, hallowed [i.e., honoured] be your name. Your kingdom come, your will be done on earth as it is in heaven. Give us today our daily bread. And forgive us our debts, as we also have forgiven our debtors. And lead us not into temptation, but deliver us from the evil one. [For the kingdom, the power and the glory are yours now and forever. Amen.] (Matthew 6:9–13)

PLEASE FILL IN THE FORM, TEAR OUT THE PAGE AND RETURN IT TO your facilitator. Your feedback will help improve the study for those doing it in the future. Thank you.

What prompted you to do the *Life of Jesus* study?

What were your expectations, hesitations, hopes, worries, etc., about this study?

How would you describe your knowledge of Jesus and/or level of Christian commitment prior to the study?

In what way(s) has this study helped your knowledge of Jesus and/or level of Christian commitment?

Would you say that you are a "Christian" (someone who has experienced repentance for the forgiveness of sins)? Why or why not?

What significant questions about the Christian faith remain for you?

What were the best things about the study?

In what ways could the study be improved for future groups?

Are you interested in further small-group discussions about the Christian life?

Any further comments?

AS LEADERS OR FACILITATORS, FEEL FREE TO EMPHASISE YOUR OWN perspectives and life experiences. Here are suggestions for each session:

SESSION 1:
Share something of your own spiritual journey.

SESSION 2:
Share something of what Jesus' authority as the Christ means to you.

SESSION 3:
Share something of what it means to you to hope for God's kingdom in the future and to live for God's kingdom right now.

SESSION 4:
Share something of your own perspective on the paradox of God's judgement and mercy.

SESSION 5:
Share what trusting in Jesus' sacrificial death means to you.

SESSION 6:
Add your own perspective on Question 4: What for you is the most significant thing about the life of Jesus?

Feel free to conclude each discussion by reading the "Session Challenge," expanding and/or clarifying as you wish.

NOTES

THE WAY WE BELIEVE

1. Aristotle, *On Rhetoric* 1.2.4.

CHAPTER 1: THE GOD-QUESTION

1. *2005–2006 World Values Survey*. For methodological details and raw data see www.worldvaluessurvey.org.

2. See the full interview, including the discussion about the beliefs of infants, at: http://www.publicchristianity.com/Videos/petrovich.html.

3. "Faith in Australia," Nielsen Poll (www.nielsen-online.com/intl.jsp ?country=au), 2009.

4. "Here Comes Christmas–A National Representative Research-only Panel Survey," McCrindle Research (www.mccrindle.com.au), 2009.

5. *2005–2006 World Values Survey*.

6. Psalm 19:1–4.

7. Romans 1:20.

8. Two respected contemporary philosophers of religion are Prof Keith Ward of the University of Oxford (UK): *Why There Almost Certainly Is a God* (Lion, 2009), an entry-level book; and Prof Alvin Plantinga of the University of Notre Dame (US): *God and Other Minds: A Study of the Rational Justification of Belief in God* (Cornell University Press, 1990), an advanced book. Interviews with both scholars can be found at www.publicchristianity.org.

9. Richard Dawkins repeats the argument, complete with, "I just go one god further," in *The God Delusion* (Bantam, 2006), 53.

10. I am aware that not all religions accept the existence of a Deus. Theravada Buddhism is traditionally atheistic. It is curious, however, that Mahayana Buddhism, the largest form of Buddhism today, reintroduced the notion of gods.

11. Probably the most reliable account of Einstein's religious views (and there are some unreliable ones) comes from Max Jammer, Professor of Physics at Bar-Ilan University in Israel: *Einstein and Religion* (Princeton University Press, 1999).

12. Paul Davies, *The Mind of God: Science and the Search for Ultimate Meaning* (Simon and Schuster, 1992).

13. Dawkins, *The God Delusion*, 20. See pages 15–20 for Prof Dawkins' ambivalent discussion of Einstein and deism.

14. Dawkins seems to think that the classical philosophical arguments for the existence of the divine, such as Thomas Aquinas' "Five Ways," are attempts to prove a "supernatural god" complete with personal qualities, moral opinions, revelations and miraculous involvements. They are not. They are simply an articulation of the reasonableness of believing the universe was caused by an immense Intelligence.

Perhaps this is why Dawkins finds the arguments for God's existence so fatuous, when professional philosophers–even the atheist ones–find them quite compelling.

15. Antony Flew, *God and Philosophy* (Hutchison, 1966); *The Presumption of Atheism and Other Philosophical Essays on God, Freedom, and Immortality* (Barnes and Noble, 1976).

16. Antony Flew, *There Is a God: How the World's Most Notorious Atheist Changed His Mind* (HarperOne, 2007).

17. Flew, *There Is a God*, 155.

CHAPTER 2: THE OBVIOUS NEXT QUESTION

1. One such book I would recommend is Ravi Zacharias, *The Grand Weaver: How God Shapes Us through the Events in Our Lives* (Zondervan, 2007).

2. We know of this through a chance discovery of Dionysius' letter to the city guard. See *New Documents Illustrating Early Christianity*, vol. 9, ed. S. R. Llewelyn (Eerdmans, 2002), 42–44.

3. For a brief account of the major faiths see my *A Spectator's Guide to World Religions: An Introduction to the Big Five* (Lion, 2008; Blue Bottle Books, 2004).

4. Flew, *There Is a God*, 155.

5. Flew, *There Is a God*, 157.

6. Flew, *There Is a God*, 213.

CHAPTER 3: EVIDENCE FOR JESUS

1. See my *The Christ Files: How Historians Know What They Know about Jesus* (Zondervan, 2010); *Investigating Jesus: An Historian's Quest* (Lion Hudson, 2010).

2. See Bellarmino Bagatti's *Excavations in Nazareth*, vol. 1 (Franciscan Printing Press, 1969); James Strange, "Nazareth," in *The Anchor Bible Dictionary*, vol. 4 (Doubleday, 1992), 1050–1051.

3. See M. Avi-Yonah, "A List of Priestly Courses from Caesarea," in *Israel Exploration Journal* 12 (1962): 137–139.

4. http://www.reuters.com/article/idUSTRE5BK1UE20091221.

5. English translation from Gerd Theissen and Annette Merz, *The Historical Jesus: A Comprehensive Guide* (Fortress, 1998), 77.

6. Translation by John Jackson, *Loeb Classical Library*, vol. 322 (Harvard University Press, 1999).

7. From an interview I conducted for Australian television, now available as *The Christ Files* DVD (Zondervan, 2010).

8. Translation by Louis H. Feldman, *Loeb Classical Library*, vol. 456 (Harvard University Press, 1996).

9. Acts 21:18.

10. *Jewish Antiquities* 18.63–64. The translation is that of Louis H. Feldman, *Loeb Classical Library*, vol. 433 (Harvard University Press, 1996).

11. Graham Stanton, *The Gospels and Jesus*, second ed. (Oxford University Press, 2003), 150.

12. Theissen and Merz, *The Historical Jesus*, 93–94.

CHAPTER 4: GOSPEL TRUTH

1. E. P. Sanders, *The Historical Figure of Jesus* (Penguin, 1993), 11.

2. This has been part of the consensus of serious scholarship ever since Richard Burridge's 1992 book, *What Are the Gospels? A Comparison with Graeco-Roman*

Biography, even though some popular writers, like bishop and theologian John Shelby Spong, continue to operate with a mytho-poetic approach to the Gospels. See Spong, *Jesus for the Non-Religious* (HarperCollins, 2007).

3. Josephus, *Against Apion* 1.1.

4. Luke was an active participant in the events recounted in Acts 16:10–17; 20:5–15; 21:1–18 and 27:1—28:16, that is, between AD 49–51, 54–57 and 59–62.

5. This point was recently emphasised by Richard Bauckham in *Jesus and the Eyewitnesses: The Gospels as Eyewitness Testimony* (Eerdmans, 2006).

6. These sources are known as Q and L. Q comes from the German *Quelle*, meaning "source," and refers to the common source for Matthew and Luke. L stands for "Luke's special source." Both of these sources are now lost to us.

7. For an account of this see my *Investigating Jesus*, 106–121.

8. Dawkins, *The God Delusion*, 95.

9. On this fraught topic see the commonsense scholarship of Martin Hengel, *The Four Gospels and the One Gospel of Jesus Christ* (Trinity Press, 2000).

10. Luke uses it in both ways elsewhere in his works: Acts 18:24–25 (of the instruction of Apollos) and Acts 21:24 (of a rumour about Paul). If Theophilus were a public follower of Jesus, I suspect Luke would have used one of the other two unmistakable words for formal Christian teaching, *didaskō* and *paradidōmi*.

11. From an interview I conducted for Australian television, now available as *The Christ Files* DVD (Zondervan, 2010).

12. Dawkins, *The God Delusion*, 5.

CHAPTER 5: MORE THAN A SURNAME

1. "Third Blessing: Grace after Meals," *The Complete Artscroll Siddur: A New Translation and Anthologized Commentary* by Rabbi Nosson Scherman (Mesorah Publications, 2003), 189.

2. See David's anointing in 1 Samuel 16:10–13.

3. *Psalms of Solomon* 17.21–32. The translation is that of R. B. Wright in *The Old Testament Pseudepigrapha*, vol. 2, ed. James Charlesworth (Doubleday, 1985), 667.

4. http://abcnews.go.com/Entertainment/elton-john-jesus-super-intelligent-gay-man/story?id=9889098.

CHAPTER 6: BETWEEN GALILEE AND TIBET

1. Michel Onfray, *The Atheist Manifesto* (Arcade, 2007), xi.

2. Josephus, *Jewish War* 3.42–43. The translation is that of H. St. J. Thackeray, *Loeb Classical Library*, vol. 487 (Harvard University Press, 1997).

3. Nicholas Notovitch's original 1894 book has been republished as *The Unknown Life of Jesus Christ* (Dragon Key, 2002).

4. Much of the following explanation of Hinduism and Buddhism comes from John Dickson, *A Spectator's Guide to World Religions: An Introduction to the Big Five* (Lion, 2008; Blue Bottle Books, 2004).

5. Shirley MacLaine's book is *Out on a Limb* (Bantam, 1986). See also the apparently popular book by Elizabeth Clare Prophet, *The Lost Years of Jesus* (Summit University Press, 1988).

6. *Conspiracy Theory: Did We Land on the Moon?* (Nash Entertainment, 2001).

7. In discussing the Gnostic Gospels Richard Dawkins in *The God Delusion* (p. 96) gets confused when he says, "The Gospel of Thomas, for example, has numerous anecdotes about the child Jesus abusing his magical powers." The Gospel of Thomas has no such stories; it is a collection of Jesus' alleged "sayings." I think

he means the Infancy Story of Thomas, which has nothing to do with the Gnostic literature Dawkins is talking about at this point.

8. *The Infancy Story of Thomas* 1.1. The translation is that of Oscar Cullmann in *New Testament Apocrypha, vol. 1: Gospels and Related Writings,* ed. Wilhelm Schneemelcher (James Clarke & Co. Ltd, 1991), 439–451.

9. *The Infancy Story of Thomas* 2.3–4.

10. *The Infancy Story of Thomas* 4.1.

11. *The Infancy Story of Thomas* 5.1.

12. Luke 6:29.

13. David Flusser, "Jesus, His Ancestry and the Commandment to Love," in James Charlesworth, ed., *Jesus' Jewishness* (Crossroad, 1991), (153–176) 161.

14. On Jesus as a carpenter see John P. Meier, *A Marginal Jew: Rethinking the Historical Jesus,* vol. 1 (Doubleday, 1991), 278–285.

CHAPTER 7: THE FIRST TEMPTATION OF CHRIST

1. Josephus, *Jewish Antiquities* 18.116–119.

2. See Kurt Rudolph, "The Baptist Sects," (471–500) in *The Cambridge History of Judaism (vol. 3): The Early Roman Period,* ed. William Horbury et. al. (Cambridge University Press, 2001), 495.

3. See John P. Meier, *A Marginal Jew: Mentor, Message and Miracles,* vol. 2 (Doubleday, 1994), 116–130.

4. Christopher Hitchens, *God Is Not Great: How Religion Poisons Everything* (Twelve, 2007), 6.

5. Hitchens, *God Is Not Great,* 18.

6. John Calvin was not formally responsible for Servetus' execution (by burning) but his support was the key to the Genevan city council's decision.

7. David Bentley Hart, *Atheist Delusions: The Christian Revolution and Its Fashionable Enemies* (Yale University Press, 2009), 33–34.

8. This comes on the authority of Edward Peters, professor of Medieval History at the University of Pennsylvania and a leading authority on the topic. See his *Inquisition* (University of California Press, 1989).

9. See William Doyle, *The French Revolution: A Very Short Introduction* (Oxford University Press, 2001).

10. Hart, *Atheist Delusions,* 5.

11. Miroslav Volf, "Christianity and Violence," *Boardman Lectureship in Christian Ethics, Paper 2,* 2002, 1. http://www.repository.upenn.edu/boardman/2.

12. See http://speakingoffaith.publicradio.org/programs/einsteinethics/einstein-myopinionofthewar.shtml.

CHAPTER 8: A TEACHER AMONG TEACHERS

1. I am indebted in much of this section to the excellent account of teachers in the ancient world in Pheme Perkins' *Jesus as Teacher* (Cambridge University Press, 1990), 1–22.

2. Fritz Graf, "Pythagoras," in *The Oxford Classical Dictionary* (Oxford University Press, 2003), 1283–1285.

3. Plato *Theaetetus* 152a6–8 and *Theaetetus* 170a3–4. Protagoras' work is known only through the quotations in Plato.

4. Epicurus, *Letter to Menoeceus (Epistula ad Menoeceum)* 128. See David John Furley, "Epicurus," in *The Oxford Classical Dictionary* (Oxford University Press, 2003), 532–534.

5. Graham Stanton, "Message and Miracles" (56–71) in *The Cambridge Companion to Jesus*, ed. Marcus Bockmuehl (Cambridge University Press, 2001), 65.

6. My use of "rabbi" here is a little anachronistic because in the early first century–the time of Jesus–the term was a simple honorific meaning "sir" or "master" more than a title for a Jewish "teacher." The latter usage developed shortly after Jesus and became the customary word for an authorized Jewish teacher.

7. *Wisdom of Ben Sira* 31:19–32:6.

8. Babylonian Talmud, *Shabbat* (*b. Sabb*) 31a. The translation is that of Philip S. Alexander in "Jesus and the Golden Rule" (363–388) in *Hillel and Jesus: Comparative Studies of Two Major Religious Leaders*, ed. James H. Charlesworth and Loren L. Johns (Fortress, 1997).

9. Luke 6:31; Matthew 7:12.

10. Confucius' *Analects* 15.24. Similarly negative formulations are found in Herodotus' *Histories* 3.142; Tobit 4.15; *Letter of Aristeas* 207; Philo *Hypothetica* 7.6.

11. For a comprehensive academic treatment of the "kingdom" in Jesus' teaching see Meier, *A Marginal Jew*, vol. 2, 237–506.

12. 4Q510 (4Q Songs of the Sage).

13. *Psalms of Solomon* 17.3–4.

14. Josephus, *Jewish Antiquities* 17.271–272, 288–289; *Jewish War* 2.56, 66–68.

15. Josephus, *Jewish Antiquities* 18.4–10, 23–25.

16. Josephus, *Jewish War* 4.72.

17. Josephus, *Jewish War* 4.79.

18. *The Rule of the Community* (1QS) 1.8–10. The translation is that of Florentino Garcia Martinez and Eibert J. C. Tigchelaar, *The Dead Sea Scrolls: Study Edition, Volume One 1Q1–4Q273* (Brill, 1997).

19. David Flusser, "Jesus, His Ancestry and the Commandment to Love," in *Jesus' Jewishness*, (153–176) 173.

CHAPTER 9: SIGNS AND WONDERS

1. The amulet and this printed translation are on display at the small but highly significant Golan Archaeological Museum in Katzrin, Israel.

2. See the catalogue of sources referring to Jesus' miracles (including a discussion of Josephus) in Meier, *A Marginal Jew*, vol. 2, 617–624.

3. Josephus, *Jewish Antiquities* 18.63.

4. The full interview with Geza Vermes, from which this quotation comes, can be viewed on *The Christ Files* DVD (Zondervan, 2010).

5. James Dunn, *Jesus Remembered* (Eerdmans, 2003), 671.

6. Philostratus, *The Life of Apollonius of Tyana* 4.45. The translation is that of Christopher P. Jones, *Loeb Classical Library*, vol. 16 (Harvard University Press, 2005).

7. The overwhelming consensus of scholarship affirms Jesus' wide reputation as a healer. A bibliography of resources by leading historical Jesus scholars is available for download from this book's page on the Zondervan website (www.zondervan. com).

8. David Hume, "Of Miracles" (115–136) in *On Human Nature and the Understanding* (Macmillan, 1962), 119.

9. See further, C. Stephen Evans, *The Historical Christ and the Jesus of Faith: The Incarnational Narrative as History* (Clarendon, 1996), 143–145.

10. *Dunameis* ("powers") appears in Mark 5:30; 6:2; 6:5; 6:14; 9:39; in Q (Matthew 11:21/Luke 10:13; Matthew 11:23/Luke 10:19); and in Matthew 7:22; 11:20; and Luke 5:17; 6:19; 9:1; 10:19; 19:37. *Sēmeia* ("signs") appears in Mark 8:11; 13:22; Luke 23:8; John 2:11, 23; 3:2; 4:48; 4:54; 6:2, 4, 26; 7:31; 9:16; 11:47; 12:18, 37; 20:30. *Sēmeia* is a favourite term in John's Gospel and his source, known as the Signs Source. Other, less frequently used, terms for Jesus' baffling deeds are *terata* or "wonders" (Mark 13:22; John 4:48) and *erga* or "works" (John 5:20, 36; 7:3; 10:25; 14:11; 15:24).

11. N. T. Wright, *Jesus and the Victory of God* (Fortress, 1996), 188.

12. Dawkins, *The God Delusion*, 91. The original quotation comes from David Hume, "Of Miracles" (115–136) in *On Human Nature and the Understanding* (Macmillan, 1962), 120.

13. For those unwilling to wade through the philosophical tomes, let me point you to the brilliant online facility hosted by Stanford University in the US (mirrored by Sydney University in Australia and the University of Leeds in the UK), *The Stanford Encyclopedia of Philosophy* (http://plato.stanford.edu/contents.html).

14. Dunn, *Jesus Remembered*, 461.

15. Deuteronomy 28:15–28.

16. 4Q521. The translation is that of Florentino Garcia Martinez and Eibert J. C. Tigchelaar, *The Dead Sea Scrolls: Study Edition, Volume Two 4Q274–11Q31* (Brill, 1998).

17. Dunn, *Jesus Remembered*, 449.

CHAPTER 10: WHY DOESN'T GOD DO SOMETHING ABOUT THE MESS IN THE WORLD?

1. Brhadaranyaka Upanishad 4.4.5–6.

2. *Setting in Motion the Wheel of Truth* (Dhammacakkappavattana Sutta) Samyutta Nikaya LVI.11, from the Sutta Pitaka.

3. Quran 57:22.

4. *The Telegraph*, London, Wed May 10, 1995.

5. Revelation 21:4–5.

CHAPTER 11: HELL-FIRE AND BRIMSTONE

1. Dale C. Allison, *Jesus of Nazareth: Millenarian Prophet* (Fortress, 1998), 103.

2. Testament of Issachar 5.1–3. The translation is that of Howard C. Kee in *The Old Testament Pseudepigrapha*, vol. 1, ed. James Charlesworth (Doubleday, 1983).

CHAPTER 12: FRIEND OF SINNERS

1. *Psalm of Solomon* 3.9–12.

2. Luke 5:30; 15:1; 19:2.

3. Philo, *The Embassy to Gaius* 199. The translation is that of F. H. Colson, *Loeb Classical Library*, vol. 379 (Harvard University Press, 1991).

4. See Dunn, *Jesus Remembered*, 532–534; Sanders, *The Historical Figure of Jesus*, 227–230.

5. Joachim Jeremias, *New Testament Theology (vol. 1): The Proclamation of Jesus* (SCM, 1971), 110.

6. The Old Testament frequently defends the cause of the poor against the rich: e.g., Exodus 2:23; Leviticus 19:13; Deuteronomy 24:14–15; Jerermiah 22:13.

7. Ben Sira 9.16.

8. Ben Sira 11.29.

9. Ben Sira 13.16–17.

10. On the Essene view of table fellowship see, E. P. Sanders, *Judaism: Practice and Belief, 63 BCE—66 CE* (SCM, 1992), 352–357; James Dunn, "Jesus, Table-Fellowship and Qumran" (254–272) in *Jesus and the Dead Sea Scrolls*; and Dunn, *Jesus Remembered*, 603–605.

11. 1QS 6.24. The translation is that of Florentino Garcia Martinez and Eibert J. C. Tigchelaar, *The Dead Sea Scrolls: Study Edition, Volume One 1Q1–4Q27* (Brill, 1997).

12. Josephus, *Jewish War* 2.129–144.

CHAPTER 13: JESUS ON SIN, GOD AND RELIGION

1. Onfray, *The Atheist Manifesto*, 67.

2. Mark 7:1–8.

3. Alain de Botton, *Status Anxiety* (Hamish Hamilton, 2004).

4. Hart, *Atheist Delusions*, 24–25.

5. Alistair McFadyen, *Bound to Sin: Abuse, Holocaust and the Christian Doctrine of Sin* (Cambridge University Press, 2000).

CHAPTER 14: A BRIEF HISTORY OF CRUCIFIXION

1. Martin Hengel, *Crucifixion: In the Ancient World and the Folly of the Message of the Cross* (Fortress, 1977).

2. Sometimes feeding to wild beasts took the place of decapitation. Hengel, *Crucifixion*, 33.

3. Hengel, *Crucifixion*, 22–23.

4. Hengel, *Crucifixion*, 39–51.

5. Josephus, *Jewish Antiquities* 17.295.

6. Josephus, *The Jewish War* 5.451.

7. Jannaeus' actions are utterly condemned by Josephus in *Jewish War* 1.97.

8. Hengel, *Crucifixion*, 87. See, for example, the first-century writing by Chariton, *Callirhoe* 4.2.6–7.

9. Seneca *Dialogue* 6 (De consolatione ad Marciam) 20.3. See Hengel, *Crucifixion*, 25.

10. Seneca, *Epistles* 101.14.

11. The definitive report of the find is J. Zias and E. Sekeles, "The Crucified Man from Giv'at ha-Mivtar: A Reappraisal," *Israel Exploration Journal* 35 (1985): 22–27.

12. Hengel, *Crucifixion*, 87.

13. Josephus, *Jewish War* 4.317.

14. The burial of Jesus is attested in Mark 15:42–47 (repeated in Matthew 27:57–61 and Luke 23:50–55) and independently in John 19:38–42. Furthermore, the apostle Paul, independently of all four Gospels, mentions that Jesus "was buried" (1 Corinthians 15:4).

15. John Dominic Crossan, *The Historical Jesus* (Harper San Francisco, 1991), 372, emphasis added.

16. *Jewish Antiquities* 18.63–64.

17. Spong, *Jesus for the Non-Religious*, 115.

18. Spong, *Jesus for the Non-Religious*, 108.

19. Mark 14:50.

20. Mark 14:54.

21. Mark 10:46.

22. Mark 5:22 and Luke 8:41.

23. Ancient Jewish comments about the testimony of women are found in: Josephus, *Jewish Antiquities* 4.219; Mishnah *Shabuot* 4.1.

24. See the excellent treatment of the issue in Bauckham, *Jesus and the Eyewitnesses*, 48–51.

25. Dunn, *Jesus Remembered*, 779.

CHAPTER 15: THE REASONS FOR JESUS' DEATH

1. Dunn, *Jesus Remembered*, 784.

2. Mark 6:17–29; repeated in Matthew 14:3–12.

3. Josephus, *Jewish Antiquities* 18.118.

4. Jeremias, *New Testament Theology (vol. 1)*, 278. Sorcery is condemned in the Old Testament (Deuteronomy 18:9–12). The Mishnah makes it one of the crimes punishable by stoning: *Sanhedrin* 7.4.

5. Mark 12:13 is the last reference to the Pharisees. The priests appear frequently from then on: Mark 14:1, 10, 43, 53, 55; 15:1, 3, 10–11, 31. A similar pattern can be observed in the other three Gospels as well.

6. Paula Fredriksen, *Jesus of Nazareth: King of the Jews* (Vintage, 1997), 242.

7. E. P. Sanders, *Jesus and Judaism*, 305.

8. Josephus, *Jewish War* 6:300–309.

9. *Temple Scroll* (11Q19). Another Jewish text likewise speaks of God's replacement of the Jerusalem temple with a more glorious one, *1 Enoch* 90.28–29. Though probably not a text produced by the Essenes, a copy of *1 Enoch* was discovered amongst the Dead Sea Scrolls. The Qumran community obviously liked what they read in it.

10. The precise dimension of the Essenes' hoped-for temple are laid out in the *Temple Scroll* (11Q19) 30–42.

11. See Otto Betz, "Jesus and the Temple Scroll" (75–103) in *Jesus and the Dead Sea Scrolls*, 100.

12. See also Sanders, *The Historical Figure of Jesus*, 272–273.

13. Indeed, it was customary for the Roman prefect, with additional troops, to be present in Jerusalem during Passover precisely to quash any excited Jews with notions of divine liberation. See Sanders, *Judaism*, 137–138. Josephus records that during one Passover thousands of worshippers were killed by the Romans for starting a riot: Josephus, *Jewish Antiquities* 20.106–112.

14. Philo, *The Embassy to Gaius* 302.

CHAPTER 16: JESUS' VIEW OF HIS DEATH

1. Many of the gravestones at the Anzac memorial on the Gallipoli Peninsula contain this saying. It comes originally from the King James Version of John 15:13.

2. Birger Gerhardsson, *The Reliability of the Gospel Tradition* (Hendrickson, 2001); Henry Wansbrough, ed., *Jesus and the Oral Gospel Tradition* (Sheffield Academic Press, 1991).

3. On Paul as a bearer of the oral tradition of those before him see Gerhardsson, *The Reliability of the Gospel Tradition*, 16–25.

4. Galatians 1:18–20.

5. Dunn, *Jesus Remembered*, 855.

6. Again, the Graeco-Roman texts are too numerous to list, but they are conveniently gathered together in chapter 1 of the very important study of the topic by Martin Hengel, *The Atonement: The Origins of the Doctrine in the New Testament* (Wipf and Stock, 1981), 1–32. It is often wrongly thought that Hinduism has always shunned

the notion of atoning sacrifice. However, the Vedas, the earliest texts of Hinduism (1500–500 BC), contain numerous unambiguous references to the early Hindu practice of offering an animal on behalf of human sin (see Rig-veda 1.1; 1.26; 1.163; 10.56).

7. Quran 6:164.

8. Quran 2:271; Hadith, Al-Bukhari 300.

9. See Martin Hengel, *The Atonement*, 33–75; Peter Stuhlmacher, "Isaiah 53 in the Gospels and Acts" (147–162) in *The Suffering Servant: Isaiah 53 in Jewish and Christian Sources*, ed. Bernd Janowski and Peter Stuhlmacher (Eerdmans, 2004).

10. Steve Chalke, *The Lost Message of Jesus* (Zondervan, 2003), 182–183.

11. Dawkins, *The God Delusion*, 253.

CHAPTER 17: A SERIOUS QUESTION

1. Sanders, *The Historical Figure of Jesus*, 280.

2. Pinchas Lapide, *The Resurrection of Jesus: A Jewish Perspective* (Wipf and Stock, 1982), 125–126.

3. To offer just a few important volumes: S. T. Davis, ed., *The Resurrection: An Interdisciplinary Symposium on the Resurrection of Jesus* (Oxford University Press, 1998); N. T. Wright, *The Resurrection of the Son of God* (SPCK, 2003); G. Vermes, *The Resurrection* (Doubleday, 2008); and G. Lüdemann, *What Really Happened to Jesus: A Historical Approach to the Resurrection* (Westminster John Knox, 1995).

4. Matthew 28:11–15; Justin, *Dialogue with Trypho* 108.

5. Geza Vermes, *Jesus the Jew: A Historian's Reading of the Gospels* (Collins, 1973), 40.

6. Sanders, *The Historical Figure of Jesus*, 10–11.

7. Dunn, *Jesus Remembered*, 855.

8. For example, G. Lüdemann, *What Really Happened to Jesus*, 14–15; R. Funk, *The Acts of Jesus: The Search for the Authentic Deeds of Jesus* (Harper, 1998), 466.

9. The other Gospel references are Matthew 28:1–10, Mark 16:1–8 and John 20:14–18.

10. Josephus, *Jewish Antiquities* 4.219

11. *Mishnah Shabuot* 4.1.

12. Apostle John Zebedee (Acts 12:1–2); James the brother of Jesus (Josephus *Jewish Antiquities* 20.200); Peter and Paul (1 Clement 5:1–7; Eusebius Ecclesiastical History 2.25.5–6).

13. Sanders, *The Historical Figure of Jesus*, 280.

14. Vermes, *Jesus the Jew*, 40.

15. James Charlesworth, *The Historical Jesus: An Essential Guide* (Abingdon, 2008), 117.

CHAPTER 18: WHAT JESUS EXPECTED

1. Larry W. Hurtado, *How on Earth Did Jesus Become a God? Historical Questions about Earliest Devotion to Jesus* (Eerdmans, 2005). A more academic version of the argument can be found in the same author's *Lord Jesus Christ: Devotion to Jesus in Earliest Christianity* (Eerdmans, 2003).

CHAPTER 19: MOVING FORWARD

1. See Peter Harrison's *The Bible, Protestantism and the Rise of Natural Science* (Cambridge University Press, 1998); and more recently *The Fall of Man and the Foundations of Science* (Cambridge University Press, 2007).

2. Jürgen Habermas, *Time of Transitions* (Polity, 2006), 150–51.